T0322816

MANCHESTER'S SHIP CANAL

THE BIG DITCH

NAVIGATION AND COMMERCE

THE MANCHESTER SHIP CANAL COMPANY

MANCHESTER'S SHIP CANAL
THE BIG DITCH

CYRIL WOOD

This book is dedicated to my brother Jim

Frontispiece: The MSC crest.

This book was first published in 2005 by Tempus Publishing
Reprinted in 2006

Reprinted in 2008 by
The History Press
The Mill, Brimscombe Port,
Stroud, Gloucestershire, GL5 2QG
www.thehistorypress.co.uk

Reprinted 2010, 2011, 2012

© Cyril Wood, 2005

The right of Cyril Wood to be identified as the Author
of this work has been asserted in accordance with the
Copyright, Designs and Patents Act 1988.

All rights reserved. No part of this book may be reprinted
or reproduced or utilised in any form or by any electronic,
mechanical or other means, now known or hereafter invented,
including photocopying and recording, or in any information
storage or retrieval system, without the permission in writing
from the Publisher.

British Library Cataloguing in Publication Data.
A catalogue record for this book is available from the British Library.

ISBN 978 07524 2811 6

Printed and bound in England.

Contents

Acknowledgements

I would like to thank my wife Angie for her encouragement and perseverance while I was working on yet another project; for her invaluable help in making the manuscript 'readable'; and for 'taking a turn' with the proof-reading. I would also like to thank my brother, Jim, for his help with the text proof-reading; Alan Savage for checking the maps for accuracy; Mike Webb of Peel Holdings – the MSC's owners – for providing invaluable geographical and historical information; the staff at the Greater Manchester Records Office for allowing access to the MSC's photographic archives; Halton Borough Council for supplying the computer generated images of the Second Mersey Crossing; Steve Cropper and the library staff of Wirral Metropolitan College's Carlett Park Campus at Eastham; as well as friends and fellow canal enthusiasts who have contributed so much information and additional photographs for publication.

Introduction

I was most surprised when Tempus Publishing contacted me regarding the publication of a second edition of *The Big Ditch* as it had only been eighteen months since it was first published.

Following the success of my previous book *The Duke's Cut: The Bridgewater Canal* it seemed logical to produce a companion book on its sister waterway, the Manchester Ship Canal, or as it is more fondly referred to 'The Big Ditch'. The histories of the two waterways are linked in many ways as is the geography and the sharing of their ultimate destination; the City of Manchester.

The Big Ditch: The Manchester Ship Canal documents the history and geography of one of the most successful of our inland waterways. The completion of this waterway lead to the City of Manchester being the largest inland port in this country and contributed towards the prosperity of not only the city but the country as well. Throughout the text of this book the Manchester Ship Canal is abbreviated to 'MSC'.

If you look at any map of the MSC's route you will see the remains of the many waterways that were connected with it in some way (both in the physical and historical sense). The area around Warrington is especially rich in disused cuts, meanders in the River Mersey no longer used and canals that either pre-empted the MSC or connected with it.

This book is split-up into three chapters; the History, the Geography and Navigational Information, and provides both historical and contemporary portraits of the MSC in text and photographs. There have been many publications on the MSC and each book has its own individuality and focuses on different aspects of the subject. As far as I am aware, this is the first book that documents the canal with the aforementioned text and photographs as well as up to date and accurate maps. I have tried to produce a book that concentrates on the 'mechanics' of the canal's history and geography concisely and without the encumbrance of facts that the reader usually skips. It was written by a canal enthusiast for canal enthusiasts as well as local historians, industrial archaeologists and other interested parties.

I hope that you, the reader, find this book a readable, informative and entertaining piece of work that relates the MSC's history, describes its route, gives invaluable information to those wishing to use it and cruise it. Many of the features and locations that were once familiar have disappeared or have changed beyond recognition. Some of these features have been described and photographed for future generations. I also hope that the book refreshes forgotten memories for readers that knew the MSC as it was in its heyday and gives a new perspective to the readers who have never visited it or only know these features as they are today.

The contemporary photographs in this book were taken by myself and the remainder from the Greater Manchester Records Office, Wirral Metropolitan College's Carlett Park Library and the many friends and fellow canal enthusiasts who entrusted their valuable photographs to me for scanning, for which I am most grateful. The photographs that I took were taken on many types of cameras and so their technical quality, especially those taken on large and meduim format cannot be appreciated when reproduced in a book, even when using modern digital scanning and printing techniques.

I apologise beforehand for any inaccuracies that may have crept in to the text or maps. No doubt, I will have omitted some details, incidents or happenings that would have been worthy of inclusion, for this I also apologise but you can always contact me via Tempus Publishing and I'll try to include the corrections or additional information in any subsequent editions!

Cyril J Wood
November 2006

one

The History of the Canal

The history of the MSC can be traced back many thousands of years to the Stone Age. When the MSC was being constructed in the 1890s, dugout canoes were discovered at two locations throughout its length where a river previously existed. While the owners of these canoes could not have had any direct bearing on the canal as it is today, their discovery may indicate that the importance of the rivers Mersey and Irwell was recognised when mankind was in its infancy.

The first purpose-built inland navigations in England can be attributed to the Romans. They constructed navigable cuts known as 'fosses' or 'dykes' on some of our rivers to bypass navigational hazards. Three of the better known of these cuts are the Caer Dyke, the Fosse Dyke and the Itchen Dyke.

The Carr (or Caer) Dyke ran from the river Witham at Lincoln to Peterborough; the Fosse Dyke also ran from the Witham at Lincoln but connected the town with the river Trent; the Itchen Dyke ran from Winchester to the sea. No doubt, these artificial waterways were monumental in the development of the Lincoln area as a Roman stronghold.

Over successive centuries, there have been other attempts to produce workable navigations, some of which became successful and still survive today. The erroneously named Exeter Ship Canal (which could only accommodate barges, not ships), constructed in 1566 by John Trew, ran alongside the river Exe. It was originally constructed to bypass a section of the river Exe notorious for shoals and scours, connecting Exeter to the sea. This navigation features the first pound locks (as against flash locks) in England.

The invention of the pound lock is often attributed to Leonardo Da Vinci, but there have been locks of this type in Holland since the fourteenth century, and previously, the Grand Canal in China, well before Da Vinci's birth.

One of the busiest natural inland waterways in the country was the river Severn. It is not surprising that it should figure somewhere in the development of the inland waterways system. Two notable navigations connected to the Severn are the Dick Brook and the (Worcestershire) River Stour Navigation, both built by Andrew Yarrington. These navigations provided transport of raw materials and finished articles to and from the industrial areas that sprouted along the banks of the Severn. The Dick Brook is notable as being a small stream near Stourport that was made navigable to access Yarrington's foundry and workshops, and possessed some of the earliest pound locks constructed in this country.

The river Thames had also been modified with flash locks at first, and pound locks in later years. A waterway connecting with the river Thames, the river Lee, now part of the Lee and Stort Navigation, has the distinction of being the first waterway in

England to apply for an Act of Parliament, in 1424, to allow improvements for navigation. Although not directly concerned with inland navigation, the last addition to the Thames was the Thames Barrier, a movable tidal and surge flood barrier constructed at Woolwich in 1982. It is the largest movable flood barrier in the world, spanning 520m (⅓ mile).

It is interesting to note that a tidal barrier, or barrage, complete with sea locks, hydro-electric power plants and a dual carriageway across the top, has been proposed on many occasions to span the river Mersey estuary between Wallasey and Liverpool. Unfortunately, the scheme has never progressed past the planning stage due to a number of reasons, the main ones being cost; damage to the river's scouring (self-dredging) effect; and ecological concerns regarding the wildlife on the river's marshes and mudflats upstream from Eastham where the MSC starts.

There has always been a natural water connection between Manchester and the Irish Sea via the rivers Irwell, Irk, Medlock and Mersey. Although this connection was not necessarily always a navigable one, over the years it has been modified by subsequent generations to provide passage for the craft of that time.

A painting depicting the river Irwell at Barton Locks with Brindley's aqueduct in the background. It is interesting to compare the painting with the photograph from the same location on page 39.

The Romans were the first to realise the importance of river navigation in the area, and must have experienced considerable difficulty navigating the river Mersey, especially between Warrington and Manchester where successive loops or meanders in the river almost doubled back on themselves. They concentrated on the building of roads to aid communication in the area, and their input into making the river more easily navigable was centred around the Castlefield area of Manchester, so-called because of the vicinity of the fort they had established there. In 84AD, they constructed a fosse or navigable cut to connect the rivers Irk and Irwell, upstream from where the river Medlock joins the Irwell. Little is known or documented about the craft that navigated the Irwell and Mersey at this time, or the type of cargo carried, but I think that it is safe to assume that Roman galleys never made it as far upstream as Castlefield.

Little did the Romans know that, in the construction of this fosse, they were laying the foundation stones for future generations of waterways, navigations and canals in this area. The development of these waterways was to have a profound affect on transport in this country at the start of the Industrial Revolution, and would eventually create the largest inland port in Great Britain. Unfortunately, no remains of the Castlefield fosse survive, although the remains of the castle have been rebuilt into a tourist attraction.

The Roman fort was inhabited for 300 years before the Romans moved on and their place was taken by the Anglo-Saxons. The Romans had quite an influence on the area,

An early photograph of a Mersey and Irwell Navigation lock. This one was located near what is now Mode Wheel on the outskirts of Manchester. Note the gas lamp to aid night-time navigation.

including the construction of a ford at Stretford. The ford was used by the trains of packhorses that provided the mainstay for the transportation of goods at that time. The ford was well used and remained in existence until 1226, when it was replaced by a bridge.

From Medieval times, navigation on the river Mersey was controlled by millers who had constructed dams across the river to maintain a sufficient head of water to turn the water wheels that powered their mills, and fishermen who also constructed weirs across the river to retain fish for ease of capture. If craft wished to pass one of these dams, they had to navigate through temporary gaps in these weirs known as flash locks.

The passage of the flash lock was a dangerous procedure and very wasteful of water. When navigating a flash lock, a gate would be opened and, if navigating downstream, the water passing through the gap in the dam would 'flush' the craft through. When navigating upstream, craft had to be towed or winched through the gap against the flow of water. Both manoeuvres were dangerous, especially when the river was in flood, and consequently, many sailors were injured or even killed, as well as craft being lost or damaged. Accordingly, passage was not actively encouraged in order to maintain a sufficient head of water in the millraces, to ensure operation of the water wheels and the retention of fish stocks retained by the dam.

The first reference to the possibility of making a more direct water route between Liverpool and Manchester came in 1697 when Thomas Patten of Bank Hall, Warrington, remarked in a letter to another businessman, Richard Norres of Speke near Liverpool, about how beneficial it would be to remove all the weirs on the river Mersey upstream of Warrington, install locks and allow consistent and safe navigation to Manchester. Patten is reputed to have made a start on the project below Warrington, allowing 2,000 tons of merchandise a year to be transported to Warrington by water.

Most rivers and navigations have their own type of craft that is peculiar to the area. The Thames had its lighters; the Severn had its trows; the Humber had its keels. The Mersey was not exempt from this trend and the craft indigenous to the river were called flats. They were capable of navigating the tidal waters of the Mersey and Dee Estuaries as well as coastal journeys, and occasionally ventured as far as the Isle of Man and even over to Ireland. The usual setup was for a gaff rig fore and aft, although this design varied. Sails were also used on inland waterways when conditions allowed, although their masts had to be dropped to allow passage beneath bridges. When sails were not practical, either due to weather or other conditions, the flats were usually towed by teams of men, or, in later years, horses or tugs.

The design of the Mersey flat was shared with the Weaver flat, the craft most commonly seen on that waterway. At first, the flats could accommodate up to 20 tons of cargo but over the years, as the depth of water was increased, their draft and capacity was increased to 100 tons. The river Weaver, having a greater depth, would allow deep-drafted flats of up to 200 tons capacity.

Even though the tonnage carried by the flats varied, their physical dimensions (disregarding draft) remained the same at 14ft by 60ft. It was this size that was to define the dimensions of subsequent locks built not only on the Mersey and Irwell Navigation, but on most of the waterways that were eventually constructed and connected to it, such as the St Helens Canal, the Leeds and Liverpool Canal and the Rochdale Canal. In later years, it was not uncommon for flats to cross the Pennines to reach destinations as far away as Leeds, Rochdale and Sowerby Bridge. Other waterways, such as the river Douglas, the Lancaster Canal, the Chester Canal and the Wirral Line of the Ellesmere Canal were also capable of passing flats. The Bridgewater Canal only had locks at Runcorn and at Hulme in Manchester, so for general navigation length was not a problem, except for access to the canal. James Brindley had the foresight to build locks with a length of 72ft on canals that he constructed, allowing the passage of the 70ft-narrowboats that were to arrive on the scene a little later.

There is quite a lot of conjecture concerning the dimensions of the narrowboat but the generally accepted reasoning behind the 6ft 10in beam by 70ft length is that the 10 to 1 length to beam ratio produced less wash, especially when the craft was fully laden. The locks to accommodate narrowboats were also less expensive to construct (as were other canal features such as bridges, aqueducts, tunnels and so on) in addition, in the case of locks, to using less water. The average 14ft by 72ft lock requires approximately 28,000 gallons to fill it whereas a narrow lock, being half the width, requires half that volume of water.

As we have seen, Thomas Patten is accredited for the first steps towards making the Mersey navigable. However, in 1712, Thomas Steers, who was responsible for the construction of the Newry Canal in Ireland, Liverpool's first docks and improvements to the river Weaver, made a survey of the rivers Mersey and Irwell that would allow unimpeded navigation for craft to Manchester. Following his suggestions, a group of businessmen, referred to as the 'Undertakers', formed the Mersey and Irwell Navigation Co. (unofficially known as the 'Old Quay Co.' due to its location at Old Quay in Warrington). In 1721 they applied to Parliament for an Act to allow the navigation's construction. The Act was passed and construction commenced, but the project was hampered due to lack of finance.

The raising of the river Irwell's water levels caused difficulties associated with crossing the river. Bridges had to be replaced with new ones featuring arches possessing greater headroom, which would allow the passage of boats larger than previously encountered on the river. Similarly, fords had to be replaced. Notably, Trafford Ford had to be replaced with a free ferry. These problems plus the lack of finance prolonged construction, and the navigation was not completed until 1736 when craft could navigate as far as Blackfriars Bridge in Manchester. Four years later, in 1740, the navigation was extended to Hunt's Bank, which is still the head of navigation today.

In 1757, Francis Egerton proposed the building of a canal from his coal mines at Worsley near Manchester. Along with John Gilbert, the mine's agent and engineer, he wanted to solve the two main problems associated with the mine. They were of transportation of the coal and mine drainage. At that time, the coal was carried by cart or packhorse to the Mersey and Irwell Navigation, where exorbitant charges were made to transport the coal to Manchester, its main market.

Together, he and Gilbert resurrected Scroop Egerton's earlier idea for a canal, expanded upon it to incorporate an elaborate drainage system for the mines and

Brindley's original Barton Aqueduct carrying the Bridgewater Canal over the Mersey and Irwell Navigation. Note the Mersey Flat negotiating the left-hand arch which led to Barton Lock.

started to survey the route. The proposed canal would not only provide transportation for the coal and solve the problem of the mine's drainage, it would bring down the price of Worsley coal in Manchester, thus making it a more competitive and affordable commodity for the less affluent members of Manchester's population.

Brindley soon completed the survey and in 1759 an Act of Parliament was passed enabling the canal to be built. The proposed route was to run from the mines at Worsley to the Mersey and Irwell Navigation at Salford Quay, with a branch to Hollins Ferry also on the Mersey and Irwell, 9.6km (6 miles) below Barton Bridge. On 1 July 1759, work on the canal commenced, but in November that year the Salford Quay terminus was dropped in favour of Dolefield, and an additional Act of Parliament was obtained. Later, in 1763, the proposed terminus was changed yet again to Castlefield at the end of Deansgate in Manchester, and even today the canal terminates there, close to the junction with the later Rochdale Canal.

Several engineering hurdles had been crossed and the canal had reached a major obstacle, the Mersey and Irwell Navigation. Initially, a flight of locks were planned to lower the canal down to the Irwell with another flight to raise it up on the other side. This would have used too much of the canal's water resources so Brindley planned to bridge the river using a masonry aqueduct (the stone being waste, obtained from the Worsley Mines) lined with puddled clay (wet clay kneaded like dough) to make it waterproof. An Act of Parliament enabling the aqueduct's construction was passed and, on 17 July 1761, water was admitted to the completed Barton Aqueduct, which opened the Bridgewater Canal from Worsley to Stretford on the outskirts of Manchester.

The tidal river Mersey at Warrington in around 1985, with Walton Lock on the Mersey and Irwell Navigation (later connecting to the MSC) in the distance.

Barton Aqueduct was a three-arched masonry structure, 183m (600ft) long, 11m (36ft) wide and 12m (39ft) high. Scepticism was rife prior to its opening. It was given the nickname 'Castle in the Air', and many people thought that it would surely collapse when water was admitted. Needless to say, Brindley proved the sceptics wrong although there was a problem when one of the arches started to bulge. This necessitated the drainage of the aqueduct after the opening ceremonies, but it was soon rectified and the canal was open to through traffic. The Bridgewater Canal was a great success and its route was later continued to Runcorn, where it connected to the river Mersey by locks. The Bridgewater Canal's story is documented in *The Duke's Cut: The Bridgewater Canal*, published by Tempus Publishing.

Another canal that started in the Runcorn locality was the Runcorn and Latchford Canal, which was opened in 1804. As its name suggests, it ran from Runcorn, 2km upstream from where the Bridgewater Canal connected with the river Mersey, to Latchford Lock, at Warrington on the Mersey and Irwell Navigation.

The lower reaches of the canal can still be traced in the marshland at Runcorn between the Ship Canal and the Mersey, opposite Fiddler's Ferry Power Station and in the area around Moore, close to the Crossfield chemical complex. The upper reaches were either absorbed into the Ship Canal's route or obliterated during its construction.

The original Woolston Cut near Lymm was built to bypass one of the many meanders in the river Mersey in the Warrington area. In 1821 it was supplemented

An in-filled lock on what was the Mersey and Irwell Navigation in Warrington.

The now disused Hulme Lock, connecting the Bridgewater Canal to the river Irwell above Manchester Docks.

Barges moored on the 'Black Bear Canal', part of the Mersey and Irwell Navigation in Warrington, during the 1920s.

with Woolston New Cut, which cut off even more of the meander and made the route to Manchester more direct by eliminating about 2km of the original route. Traces of the original Woolston Cut and the meander that it replaced can still be seen, but parts of it have silted up over the years.

The year 1822 saw a proposal for a railway from Manchester to Liverpool. Right from the outset, the Mersey and Irwell Navigation Co. and the Bridgewater Canal Co. both opposed its development, seeing the far-reaching repercussions it would have on their waterway.

In an effort to make its route more comprehensive, two extension plans to the Bridgewater Canal were drawn up. The first, in 1823, proposed an extension from Sale to Stockport but was thwarted due to oppositions from the Ashton and Peak Forest Canals. The second plan, two years later, was far more ambitious. It was for a canal, possibly of ship-canal dimensions, to link Runcorn, on the Mersey, with West Kirby, on the river Dee coast of the Wirral Peninsula. This plan was thrown out for many reasons, the major one being cost.

It is possible that the latter plan was to have been executed by Thomas Telford who, coincidentally, later carried out a survey to construct a ship canal from Wallasey Pool to West Kirby and so bypass the river Mersey estuary, which contained many navigational hazards. Telford is reported to have said about Liverpool, 'Look... they've built the docks on the wrong side of the river'. He made this comment due to Wallasey Pool, the location of today's Wallasey and Birkenhead Docks, being a natural harbour as against Liverpool's docks, many of which are constructed within reclaimed land. Had his plan been successful, Liverpool would undoubtedly, not have had the successes that it ultimately enjoyed, and the MSC as we know it today would not have been built.

The year 1838 saw the building of the Hulme Lock branch of the Bridgewater Canal. This branch connected the Bridgewater Canal to the river Irwell, adjacent to where the Medlock runs into the Irwell. The Hulme Lock branch superseded the previous connection with the Irwell at Cornbrook known as 'The Gut'.

Despite the modernisation of cargo-handling facilities on the Bridgewater Canal and a toll war with the Mersey and Irwell Navigation, the railways were having a noticeable affect on the tonnages carried along both waterways. One logical solution to the problem would be for the Bridgewater Canal Co. to control trade on the Mersey and Irwell Navigation. Consequently, an Act enabling the Bridgewater Canal Co. to purchase the shares of the Mersey and Irwell was passed, and the transfer of shares took place on 17 January 1846. The sum paid for the navigation was £550,000.

While the acquisition of the Mersey and Irwell Navigation no doubt helped to boost both waterways' financial position in the face of the railways, they still needed to be competitive. By 1860, the Mersey and Irwell was so silted-up that it was impossible for all but the shallowest drafted craft to reach Manchester unless there was an abundance of 'fresh' coming down the river Irwell and the river Mersey. Consequently, in 1872, a new company was formed to inject capital necessary for the dredging of the Mersey and Irwell and increased warehousing, as well as new cargo-handling equipment on the Bridgewater Canal, and included the purchase of steam tugs after their successful trials had been completed. The new company was called the 'Bridgewater Navigation Co. Ltd'. It is ironical that many of the shareholders also held shares in railway companies and, that the body collecting shares for the trustees of the company was actually a collection of railway companies.

During the nineteenth century there were many proposals for schemes to build a new canal to Manchester. In 1838, Sir John Rennie, the celebrated engineer and canal builder, was commissioned to make a survey of the Mersey and Irwell Navigation. His conclusions were that a completely new canal would be preferable to modifying the existing Mersey and Irwell. Following on from this, two years later, H.R. Palmer was instructed by the Mersey and Irwell Navigation Co. to prepare plans for the scheme. In order to ensure the best scheme possible, John H. Bateman was also commissioned to produce an alternative plan. Both routes started at Runcorn Gap and utilised part of the existing waterways. Eventually, the proposals were dropped, mainly due to problems surrounding the raising of sufficient capital to finance such a scheme.

It was nearly forty years later, in 1877, that Hamilton Fulton proposed yet another scheme for a new canal to supersede the Mersey and Irwell Navigation. Fulton proposed a canal of larger dimensions than those of the Mersey and Irwell, to allow large, ocean-going ships to reach Manchester. In 1882, Daniel Adamson, a Manchester engineer, introduced Fulton to a group of influential businessmen – the mayors of towns through which his proposed canal would pass and financiers interested in becoming involved with the project.

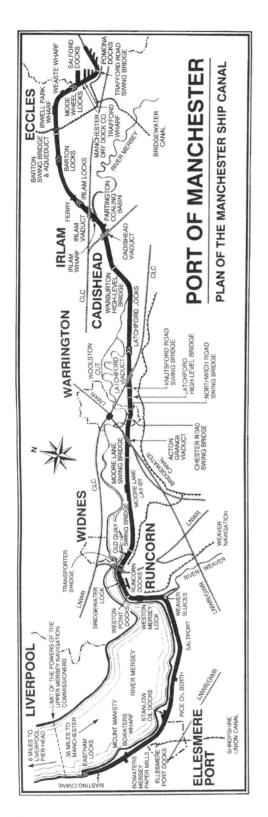

PORT OF MANCHESTER

PLAN OF THE MANCHESTER SHIP CANAL

Above: *An early unclear map (undated but probably Rennie's survey of 1838), showing the route of the proposed ship canal from Runcorn (not Eastham) to Manchester. The map also shows the start of a proposed canal from Ellesmere Port to the river Dee estuary.*

Left: *The second, more contemporary, map shows the MSC's eventual route.*

This undated photograph shows the MSC Walton – a Bridgewater Canal tug on the MSC at an unidentified location.

An undated photograph showing a narrowboat crossing Brindley's original Barton Aqueduct. Note the calm water beneath the left-hand arch leading to Barton Lock beyond.

Left: *Daniel Adamson, the father of the Manchester Ship Canal.*

Below: *Temporary bridges were erected to allow access from one side of the workings to the other, without the need to go down one side and up the other. These would have been especially beneficial when pushing a wheelbarrow.*

Opposite: *Construction work at Eastham, looking towards Mount Manisty, probably around 1891.*

The proposed scheme was for the building of a ship canal from Eastham on the Wirral bank of the river Mersey estuary to a large purpose-built dock complex at Manchester, close to the racecourse. The canal would be following the same general route as the Mersey and Irwell Navigation from Runcorn to Manchester, with several new cuts and extensions plus a completely new section from Eastham to Runcorn, effectively hugging the banks of the river Mersey, and separated from the tidal estuary by an embankment. The canal was to be 35 miles in length and 60½ ft above sea level by the time it reached Manchester. The differences in levels were overcome by the construction of locks situated at Eastham, Latchford, Barton and Mode Wheel.

The proposed plan caused much excitement and many people wanted to become involved in a scheme that they thought would bring added prosperity to Manchester. After the preliminary survey for the route, plans were formulated for the raising of the necessary capital. On the negative side, the plan was vigorously opposed by many groups, including the city of Liverpool, which was afraid that the competition generated by a ship canal would adversely affect the city's livelihood.

In 1883, The Manchester Ship Canal Act had its first reading in Parliament. It was passed by the House of Commons but thrown out by the House of Lords. The following year, 1884, the Act was again submitted to Parliament and was passed by the House of Lords but thrown out by the House of Commons. This failure caused much disdain in Manchester but the promoters did not lose faith in their dream, and submitted their proposal to Parliament a third time. It was a case of 'third time lucky' as it was passed by both houses in 1885. The same year, the Manchester Ship Canal Co.

bought the Bridgewater Navigation Co. Ltd, which had turned out to be a fairly short-lived company.

The next couple of years were spent on preparations for the canal's construction, obtaining the land through which the canal was to be built, purchasing digging equipment and materials, organising the workforce and so on. A contractor was also appointed. This was Thomas Walker, an experienced civil engineering contractor, famous for the construction of the Severn Tunnel for the Great Western Railway. At the Jubilee Exhibition of 1887, a scale model of the proposed canal was on display, and aroused interest from all over the world. With the preparations well in hand, Lord Egerton cut the first sod of earth on 11 November 1887 at the site of the entrance locks at Eastham.

The following year, construction started in earnest. The route was split up into eight sections: 1.) Eastham to Ellesmere Port; 2.) Ellesmere Port to Ince; 3.) Ince to Weston Point; 4.) Weston Point to Norton; 5.) Norton to Latchford; 6.) Latchford to Warburton; 7.) Warburton to Barton; and 8.) Barton to Manchester.

Construction went well initially. Much of the excavation was performed by manual labour, and workers were recruited from all over the country to be employed as 'Navvies' to work on the canal. The manual labour was supplemented by revolutionary excavators known as 'Steam Navvies', many of which were specially imported from Germany. They were used to scrape earth out of the workings and to profile the sides of the canal bed. A railway was constructed along the length of the workings from Eastham to Manchester to supply equipment and construction materials to various locations along the large, linear construction site. This railway line was partially dismantled after construction although some of it was retained and was later to be the largest private railway complex in the country.

By the beginning of 1889, construction was well in hand but a long series of devastating blows were to affect the canal's construction and threaten the completion of the project. Daniel Adamson died in January 1889 at the age of seventy-one. Although his death did not affect construction, it did dampen morale. Shortly after this, prolonged rainstorms raised the water levels in the rivers Irwell and Mersey. In many locations, the rivers had been diverted to allow the canal's construction. Many of the temporary dams built to protect the construction work were washed away by the increased amount of water passing down the rivers, undoing many months of work.

Floods in the Latchford section between Thelwall and Lymm washed machinery away and destroyed embankments, leaving the railway lines suspended in mid-air. Between Little Bolton Cutting and Mode Wheel the temporary barrier gave way, causing 20 million gallons to flood into the works in 20 minutes. In an unrelated incident, the railway locomotives *Rhymney* and *Deal* collided head-on, killing three workmen.

In April of the same year, the Mersey Docks and Harbour Co., who had been against the construction of the ship canal from the start, served an injunction for deviating from plans regarding openings in embankments. The deviation from the original plans, they alleged, would alter the river Mersey's scouring affect, leading to the river channel at Liverpool silting up. If this proved to be correct, it would have had a devastating affect on Liverpool's trade as ships would not be able to reach the docks due to there being

The first dugout canoe discovered in 1889. This one was at Partington.

The second dugout canoe, also discovered in 1889, at Barton.

Above: *The river Mersey close to the location of the Runcorn and Latchford Canal's entrance lock at Old Quay which was demolished when the MSC was constructed.*

Left: *An undated engraving depicting Blackfriars Bridge in Manchester close to the head of navigation on the river Irwell at Hunt's Bank.*

Opposite: *The Runcorn and Latchford Canal still in water close to the demolished entrance lock at Old Quay.*

This photograph illustrates the immense size of the entrance lock gates at Eastham.

insufficient depth of water. The evidence produced was proved to be inconclusive and construction continued on the canal, unaffected by a last-minute attempt by the city of Liverpool to prevent the canal's construction.

There were some positive happenings in 1889. In Trafford Cutting, an ancient Runic Cross was unearthed by the excavations taking place there while a dugout canoe was discovered at Partington. A large quantity of Greenheart timber from British Guiana was delivered to Eastham. This was to be used in the construction of the giant 80ft entrance lock gates, which would weigh 540 tons in total. In July, the Shah of Persia visited Manchester and wished to see MSC workings. The remains of a second dugout canoe were discovered when excavations were taking place at Barton. Torrential rain and gales caused river levels to rise and breach temporary embankments, which led to 6 miles of the workings to be flooded. Later on in the year, in November, the river Irwell overflowed at Barton, causing yet more flooding and damage to the construction work. Also in November, Thomas Walker, the contractor, died aged sixty-two, and legal problems concerning his estate affected the MSC's finances and work on the canal's construction. This situation was compounded by yet more weather problems, further affecting construction. This spate of bad weather did not abate until January 1891, when remedial work could be made and normal construction recommenced.

The year 1891 did not promise to be any better for the MSC than the previous year. In February an industrial dispute over wages stopped construction. This was soon resolved but by that time financial problems were looming on the horizon.

The prolonged bad weather meant that there was a great deal of remedial work to be done. This extra work was putting a strain on the company's financial resources. Consequently, on 9 March, a special committee meeting with Manchester Corporation was called to request financial assistance. The corporation agreed to advance £3 million to the Ship Canal Co. and subsequently promoted a Bill in Parliament empowering them to do so. At a public meeting, Salford Corporation was forced by public pressure to contribute £1 million, but the decision was denied due Salford Corporation's inability to borrow that amount of money.

On 5 June 1891, 3,000 men worked around the clock to complete the Eastham section so that it could be filled with water before the ravages of the winter. Work commenced to close the gap in the embankment using concrete. Tugs and dredgers moored in the river adjacent to the gap to act as breakwaters protecting the embankment from tidal damage. Due to the construction work on this section, the regular packet steamer from Liverpool failed to dock at Ellesmere Port for the first time in fifty-four years. A £300 per day penalty was imposed on the MSC Co. due to Ellesmere Port Docks and the Shropshire Union Canal basins being inaccessible from the river Mersey until the canal was completed.

Construction machinery was removed on 18 June prior to filling. The actual date of filling this section of the canal with water was kept secret in order to prevent crowds from forming and creating a safety hazard. A hole in the embankment was made and, as the tide rose, water slowly entered the canal. The filling of the section took over a

The completed entrance lock prior to the filling of the canal, looking towards Mount Manisty.

Above: *The construction of Pool Hall Syphon which allows the river Rivacre to flow beneath the MSC close to Mount Manisty.*

Left: *The moment of truth; water is admitted into the canal at Ellesmere Port for the first time on 11 July 1891.*

Opposite: *A Bridgewater Canal tug towing a Mersey Flat through the gap in the embankment wall at Ellesmere Port, prior to the completion of the section, in order to gain access to the Shropshire Union Canal Basins at what is now the Boat Museum.*

week and, when completed, the only damage was minor landslips. However, when the hole in the embankment was filled-in with soil and hard-core on 11 July, the embankment was breached by tidal action. The following day, the breach was repaired with boulders but failed once again. It was eventually sealed with concrete on 13 July, and no further problems occurred. On the following day, at 8.45 a.m., the first ships passed along the ship canal from Eastham to Ellesmere Port. All subsequent traffic to Ellesmere Port had to go via the ship canal from Eastham.

Elsewhere along the canal, construction work was slowly being completed. On 1 August, the river Irwell was channelled into Little Barton Cutting. By 14 September, the Ince section was completed and filled with water without drama.

At the end of 1891 another financial crisis struck. An additional £863,000 was needed to complete the canal. Also, continuous rain caused the rivers Mersey and Irwell to breach embankments and flow into Irwell Cutting. At Latchford, the river Bollin also burst into the canal construction works, causing damage and demolishing machinery. At least the flooding and damage was not as bad as the previous year as only 2½ miles were flooded as against 18½ miles, but the amount of money required to complete the canal was raised to £1¼ million due to the winter flood damage.

By July 1892, the amount of money required to complete the canal was raised yet again to £2 million. Manchester Corporation raised its rates to pay the amount. Industrial unrest among workers did not help matters either but was resolved by raising wages. Cadishead Railway Viaduct at Irlam was completed, and the railway company insisted on testing its strength by driving ten railway locomotives over it, weighing a total of 750 tons. Needless to say, the viaduct passed the test with flying colours.

Above and below: *Two photographs of the river Gowy Syphon at Stanlow Island.*

Above and below: *Two photographs of the canal at Weston Point Docks on 24 April 1890, prior to filling this section of the canal. Note the church which is one of the few churches in the country built on an uninhabited island, and the now-demolished lighthouse on the upper photograph. The lower photograph shows Delamere Lock, which gave access to Runcorn Docks as well as the Bridgewater and Runcorn and Weston Canals.*

Victoria Railway Viaduct at Runcorn Gap.

Construction of Latchford Locks. Note the islands in the distance which will form the lock chambers.

Construction work above Latchford Locks.

The original Warburton Bridge over the Mersey and Irwell Navigation.

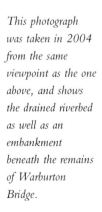

This photograph was taken in 2004 from the same viewpoint as the one above, and shows the drained riverbed as well as an embankment beneath the remains of Warburton Bridge.

Construction work on the new Warburton Bridge.

Warburton Bridge today.

Above: *The remains of the old Warburton Bridge from the road. Compare the stonework and balustrades with that on the middle photograph on page 35.*

Right: *A toll is still payable to cross Warburton Bridge. In 2005 it was 12p for a single crossing or 25p for a day ticket.*

Cadishead Railway Viaduct being tested by having ten railway locomotives being driven onto it with a combined weight of 750 tons.

Above and below: *Two photographs showing Barton Road Bridge being demolished. In the first photograph the river has been in-filled beneath the left-hand arch, and now accommodates the construction railway. In the second photograph, the centre arch has been removed and replaced by a temporary wooden roadway.*

Above and below: *Two interesting photographs from virtually the same viewpoint. In the first photograph the old Barton Lock is in the process of being demolished. Compare this shot with the painting on page 11. In the second, the lock has disappeared and an additional railway track occupies the site of the cottages.*

The construction of the Manchester Ship Canal only directly affected the Bridgewater Canal in two ways. The first was that at Runcorn; access to the river Mersey could only be gained by crossing the ship canal to Bridgewater or Old Quay Lock (further upstream), or by sailing down its length to Eastham. The second change was at the famous Barton Aqueduct. This would have to be demolished due to the limited headroom of Brindley's original structure.

Projected schemes for Barton Aqueduct's replacement included locks to lower craft to the level of the ship canal and up the opposite side (as in the Bridgewater Canal's original proposal) and a vertical lift similar to that at Anderton connecting the Trent and Mersey Canal with the river Weaver. The latter suggestion is not surprising as the lift at Anderton was the brainchild of the previous engineer for the river Weaver, who was none other than Edward Leader Williams (although it was designed and built by Edwin Clark), the engineer for the ship canal. The design that was eventually settled on was for a 'swing aqueduct'.

The swing aqueduct and the proposed swing bridges on the ship canal were to be of similar design to the road bridges that spanned the river Weaver (also designed by Edward Leader Williams). The aqueduct would pivot on an island built in the centre of the ship canal and would swing, full of water, to allow ships to pass either side. The navigation trough would be sealed at either end prior to swinging, by swinging lock-type gates to conserve water.

Its dimensions are:

Length	71.6m (235ft)
Width	5.5m (18ft)
Depth of water	1.8m (6ft)
Total weight	1,400 tons (800 tons of which is water)

The weight of the aqueduct is supported by sixty-four steel rollers, but when swung, a greased hydraulic ram takes some of the weight off the rollers. The swinging action is achieved hydraulically, being controlled from a tower on the island that overlooks both the aqueduct and the adjacent Barton Road Bridge. The aqueduct was completed in July 1893, and only then was Brindley's original structure demolished. On the northern bank of the ship canal remains to this day part of one of the buttresses and approach embankments of the original aqueduct, in addition to the site of the Barton Road Aqueduct where the road was spanned by another smaller aqueduct. Even though Brindley's original aqueduct was demolished, there remains a similar structure on the Bridgewater Canal opposite the Old Watch House at Stretford. This is the Hawthorn Lane Aqueduct and, even though built on a smaller scale, it is reminiscent of its larger brother.

Barton Aqueduct was completed on 29 May 1893, but a breach in approach to aqueduct postponed the opening and the subsequent demolition of Brindley's original aqueduct. When the breach was eventually repaired, the Bridgewater Canal could be diverted over the new aqueduct in order to maintain through traffic on the Bridgewater

The next four photographs show the swing aqueduct in various stages of construction.

Above and below: *Work demolishing Brindley's Barton Aqueduct did not commence until May 1893, when the Bridgewater Canal could be diverted across the new swing aqueduct.*

Canal and demolition of the original aqueduct could take place. When this was achieved this section of the MSC was completed. With Brindley's Barton Aqueduct out of the way, the finishing touches could be made to the MSC in preparation for its opening on 1 January 1894, having cost £14,347,891 to construct.

Heavy rain in the November of 1893 caused both the rivers Mersey and Irwell to flood into the completed, but partially filled, Runcorn to Latchford section. Within a week, the section was completed and the *Falmouth Castle*, giving a tour of the canal to directors, shareholders and local dignitaries, was the first ship to sail along its length on 25 November 1893. This section was the last to be completed and construction work on the canal was now finished from one end to the other.

With the construction work on the canal and docks at the Manchester end now completed, there were legal matters that had to be addressed. On 21 December 1893, Manchester was declared a port for customs purposes. The chairman of Salford Quarter Sessions, on 30 December of the same year, issued a certificate declaring that Manchester Docks were completed and ready to accept vessels from that day forward.

To celebrate the ship canal's completion, Manchester's streets were crowded with people welcoming in the New Year and celebrating the impending opening of the Ship Canal.

At 10.00 a.m. on 1 January 1884, a procession of vessels led by Mr Samuel Platt's yacht the *Norseman* left Eastham bound for Manchester. The Wallasey ferryboats *Crocus* and *Lupin* had been chartered by the Ship Canal Co. to carry officials, dignitaries and guests, and were among the first vessels along the canal after the *Norseman*. It is coincidental that in later years, the Mersey Ferries have offered trips along the ship canal and today are among the only regular craft to use the upper reaches of the ship canal. Also in the flotilla was the SS *Pioneer*, owned by the Co-operative Wholesale Society, which had the distinction of unloading the first cargo brought along the ship canal to Manchester.

Even though the ship canal was open for trade, it was not officially opened until 21 May 1884. Queen Victoria performed the opening ceremony by 'remote control' by throwing a switch from a console specially installed aboard the yacht *Enchantress* which activated the lock gates at Mode Wheel Locks and, in doing so, pronounced the Manchester Ship Canal officially open.

Once the passage of ships had been established, trade along the canal increased. In March 1885, the importing of cotton from the southern states of America commenced, feeding the many mills in the Lancashire area with raw materials. It was as a direct result of this trade that the shipping company Manchester Liners was formed. Their ships were to be a familiar sight on the ship canal for nearly one hundred years.

An unloading wharf was constructed at Ellesmere Port in 1899 to accommodate a large flour mill that was assembled on what was to be known as the 'Mill Arm'. Two years later, the ship *Chickahomony* brought the first bananas, mangos, oranges, rum, coconuts and logwood to Manchester. Immediately after this, a two-way service started between the Caribbean and Manchester, taking finished goods and various cargoes to the Caribbean on the return journey. To meet the increase in demand for docking

Construction work close to the location of Trafford road and rail Bridges.

The gigantic scale of the docks is evident by the size of the workmen in front of the steam crane.

Construction of No.9 Dock.

Part of the completed docks prior to the opening of the canal.

The flotilla of ships led by the Norseman *sailing up the canal on 1 January 1894.*

The official opening ceremony attended by Queen Victoria, held aboard the yacht Enchantress *on 21 May 1894.*

Above and below: *Two photographs of Manchester Docks just after the opening of the canal.*

space created by the additional shipping services using the MSC, a new dock ½ mile long was constructed on the site of the old racecourse, and opened in 1905 by King Edward VII. Four years later the overall depth of the MSC was increased to 28ft, allowing vessels of a deeper draught to use the canal. The increased depth was achieved by raising the level of water in the canal rather than additional excavation, which would have resulted in closing parts of the canal while the work took place.`

Even though the MSC was deemed a success, craft still travelled along the lower reaches of the river Mersey in the Warrington area. The giant Crossfields manufacturing plant expanded across the Mersey, and in 1912 a transporter bridge was constructed to carry vehicles across the river to various parts of the complex. This bridge supplemented an earlier transporter bridge built in 1902 that could only accommodate railway trucks. The earlier bridge has been demolished but the 1912 bridge is still in existence and, being one of the three remaining transporter bridges left in the United Kingdom, is a listed structure. Also in 1912, the Elders & Fyffe's banana trade moved from Manchester to Liverpool's Garston Docks.

Manchester was becoming one of the premier manufacturing cities in the country. Historically, manufacturing had concentrated around the textile industry, but the founding of Trafford Park industrial estate close to Manchester Docks brought a more diverse range of manufacturing to the city, ranging from motor vehicles when the Ford Motor Co. opened its first British factory; railway locomotives from the Vulcan Foundry which were sent all over the world; electrical equipment manufacturing from the General Electric Co.'s factory; to production of cornflakes from the famous Kellogg's factory, from which emanated the smell of cornflakes being baked, which wafted all over the Trafford Park area.

Further down the ship canal, at Ellesmere Port, excavation work commenced at Stanlow Island for the first oil tanker berth to serve the growing petro-chemical industry that was becoming established there. The new wharf was constructed on Stanlow Island, an outcrop of land jutting out into the river Mersey estuary, bordered by mudflats on the north and the outlet of the river Gowy to the south. In years gone by, there was a monastery on the island, but this was dissolved due to the buildings being ravaged by storms and the encroachment of the river. The island is only accessible by boat and is connected to the oil refinery by pipes laid beneath the canal. The new berth was not completed until 1922 and, as larger ships started to unload oil at Stanlow, the ship canal was deepened to a depth of 30ft from Eastham to Stanlow, to allow ships of up to 15,000 tons capacity to reach the oil berth in 1927. Due to the demand for petrol, oil and petro-chemical products, a second (and larger) tanker berth at Stanlow Island was completed in 1933, adjacent to the first.

During the Second World War, the Port of Manchester was instrumental in loading cargoes onto many ships destined to be sunk in the Atlantic Convoys. During the same period of time, a ship carrying whale oil shed its cargo into Manchester Docks, covering the water with a crust of emulsified oil. Boats cleared the spillage, working like icebreakers, and the workers were paid £8 per day to clear the spillage.

Stanlow Oil Refinery continued to grow, as did the size of the oil tankers that served it. The ship canal was too narrow to allow passage of these larger ships and plans were formulated to construct an additional dock at Eastham. The new dock was to be known as the Queen Elizabeth II Oil Terminal. Although primarily designed to unload petro-chemical oil products, it can also handle edible oil products. Its entrance locks are adjacent to the ship canal's main entrance locks, but there is no direct connection between the ship canal and the new dock except for a water supply regulated by sluices. Construction work was completed in January 1954 and pipelines were laid to connect the dock to the oil refinery at Stanlow. The new dock covers 19 acres, has locks capable of passing ships 245m x 30m and is able to accommodate tankers of 35,000 tons capacity, making it the largest enclosed oil dock in the United Kingdom.

At the other end of the ship canal, in the same year, expansion was taking place at Pomona Docks, Manchester, with the construction of new cargo-handling facilities for the expanding Colgate–Palmolive detergent and toiletries manufacturing complex.

At Runcorn, the old transporter bridge between Runcorn and Widnes was replaced by a modern bridge based on the design of the Sydney Harbour Bridge, and completed in 1964. The new bridge, possessing the largest span in Europe at the time, spanned Runcorn Gap, a narrowing in the river Mersey, a few hundred metres away from the site of the old transporter bridge. The new line of locks were in-filled in 1966, which left the Runcorn Arm of the Bridgewater Canal a dead-end with no connection to either the ship canal or the Runcorn and Weston Canal (and the River Weaver Navigation), access to which was gained via Runcorn Docks.

Two other new bridges crossed the ship canal. Thelwall Viaduct (1959) not only spanned the ship canal but also the Bridgewater Canal, a railway, a road and the river Mersey. It carries the M6 motorway across the Mersey Valley on lofty concrete pillars. Further along the ship canal, at Barton, another high-level bridge was constructed in 1960. This bridge originally carried the M62 Urmston Bypass, later to become the M63 and later still redesignated the M60, thus making it the only stretch of UK motorway to have three designations.

An upsurge of container traffic at Ellesmere Port necessitated the construction of a new purpose-built terminal at North Quay. It is not unusual to see ships from Russia and Japan moored next to each other while being unloaded. The quay at Ellesmere Port was also used for the import of foreign cars as well as the export of cars from production plants all over the country, including the local Vauxhall (Ellesmere Port) and Ford (Halewood, Liverpool, now Jaguar Cars) plants nearby. A fire damaged Telford's warehouses at the Ellesmere Port terminus of the Shropshire Union Canal. The damage was so great that it necessitated the complete demolition of the historic warehouses that spanned the SUC's basins. Two years later, in 1972, all the Liverpool Docks upstream of the Pier Head (the South Docks system) were closed except for Garston Docks, which were not connected to the Liverpool dock network. This closure of the South Docks did not affect the ship canal directly as the docks had lain derelict for many years. From the late 1960s, there had been a general downturn in traffic using all Liverpool Docks and this was echoed along the ship canal as the number of ship movements along the upper reaches of the canal and Manchester Docks fell to an all-time low, even though there had been significant investment in containerised cargo-handling installations.

A railway along the banks of the ship canal from Runcorn to Manchester was constructed at the same time as the canal. At one time it was part of the largest private railway in the country. The railway was used for maintenance purposes and was closed and dismantled in 1973, although sections around Trafford Park still survive and are in use today, but no longer transport cargoes to Manchester Docks.

The following year, 1974, saw the establishment of the Boat Museum at Ellesmere Port where the Shropshire Union Canal connects with the ship canal. The museum has since grown into one of the premier collections of ex-working craft and canal exhibits in the country, many of which are sited where Telford's warehouses were situated. The oil traffic from Lever Brothers' Bromborough Dock, which served the Port Sunlight complex, to the Crossfield's plant at Warrington, ceased in the same year.

Left and below: *New lock gates being towed from Old Quay Workshops, Runcorn to Eastham for installation, 1939.*

Once at Eastham, the new gates are lifted into position by the MSC's 250-ton floating crane.

An aerial photograph of Weston Point showing the river Mersey in the foreground, with the MSC behind it and the Weston Canal section of the Weaver Navigation nearest to the land.

Another aerial view with the MSC in the foreground, Runcorn Docks and the two lines of locks of the Bridgewater Canal in the centre of the photograph. Bridgewater House is on the bottom left. Note the sailing ships moored in the foreground.

The downward trend in shipping along the upper reaches of the ship canal continued, to such an extent that Manchester Docks would close within five years. Bridgewater Estates (including the Bridgewater Canal) and, shortly afterwards, the Manchester Ship Canal, including the Manchester Docks complex, was purchased by Peel Holdings in 1984.

When the docks closed, a large-scale regeneration scheme was initiated. This scheme was to convert derelict docks and warehouses into a prestigious business and upmarket housing development, starting with Salford Quays in 1985. The disused docks were converted into water features surrounding the development and included the construction of a new canal connecting with marina-style moorings. Parts of the dock complex were still in use. The graving docks, where ships were broken-up for scrap, dismantled a fleet of Russian fishing vessels and, in 1987, the Cawoods container service to Manchester doubled. The following year, Trafford Railway Swing Bridge was removed and floated into No.9 Dock, and converted into a footbridge. It was renamed Detroit Bridge. The pivot island close to Trafford Road Swing Bridge can still be seen, and is part of the Wharfside Promenade that follows the canal as far as the Imperial War Museum North.

A new vertical lift bridge was opened at Trafford Park, close to the Cerestar Wharf. The new bridge, named Centenary Bridge, carries the Parkway/M602 link road across the canal. Its span is 43m and it is the first movable bridge to be constructed over the canal for aone hundred years. The connection with the Bridgewater Canal, Hulme Lock, was also replaced in 1995 with a new lock, Pomona Lock. The new lock is situated at the end of Pomona Dock (formally Pomona No.3 Dock) at a location close to the original 1763 connection with the river Irwell at Cornbrook known as 'The Gut',

Runcorn–Widnes Transporter Bridge carried vehicles across the river Mersey and the MSC. At 305m, it had the longest span of any transporter bridge in the world, until it was demolished in July 1961.

which Hulme Lock replaced in 1838. In 1996, the Centenary Walk adjacent to the docks was opened. This took the shape of a promenade around the old docks, and new footbridges connected the docks, supplementing the original Trafford Railway Swing Bridge, which was previously relocated across the docks and converted into a footbridge. This bridge crosses the old No.9 Dock, now renamed North Bay. Much of the area was landscaped and new developments sprung up all along the Manchester Docks and river Irwell corridor. Manchester's 'Metrolink' tram network was expanded, and crosses the Irwell close to Pomona Dock. A station was built close to Pomona, an area that covers the in-filled Pomona No.1 and No.2 Docks, which is earmarked for further development, including the siting of a new marina in the remaining No.3 Dock.

The Mersey Ferries still visit the city of Manchester as part of their programme of regular trips along the ship canal. Another permanent maritime resident in the city was HMS *Bronington*. This retired minesweeper (once commanded by the Prince of Wales) was built in 1953, and was the last wooden minesweeper in the British Navy. It was moored adjacent to the Imperial War Museum North at Trafford Wharf until it was moved to the Historic Warships Collection, located in Wallasey and Birkenhead Docks, in July 2002.

It is ironic that the history of the area encompassing Manchester Docks has gone in a full circle. The area was originally the location of Manchester Racecourse. It became the docks complex when the ship canal was constructed and is now reverting to leisure

Above and below: *Two more photographs of the Runcorn–Widnes Transporter Bridge. The top photograph shows the platform or 'car' suspended by cables from the overhead gantry. The second photograph shows an MSC tug passing beneath the bridge, heading towards Old Quay.*

use with the establishment of the Lowry Art Gallery and shopping centre in 2000, adjacent to the site of the old No.9 Dock. The Imperial War Museum North opened in July 2002 at Trafford Wharf, and the nearby Trafford Centre – one of the premier shopping centres in the country – occupies an area used by industries serving the docks. The new Lowry Footbridge was constructed to connect the Imperial War Museum North with the Lowry Centre, and is a vertically lifting footbridge. This bridge was constructed as a lift bridge to accommodate larger craft wishing to pass beneath it into the area surrounding the Lowry Centre. The area has undergone many changes in character; from the hustle and bustle of the industrial era, the sadness and lethargy of the period when the docks fell into disuse to the atmosphere of hope as more of the area is developed and new buildings and amenities are constructed. It will be very interesting to see what future developments take place in this area.

In 2000, an unusual visitor to the ship canal was spotted at Eastham. A dolphin had followed a ship through the entrance locks at Eastham and was seen following the ship along the canal. It was eventually 'ushered' back into the Mersey estuary by staff using a 'gig' boat (a small boat used to take ropes from larger vessels) to continue its maritime wanderings.

Another unusual visitor to the MSC was the *Super Seacat* Irish ferry catamaran. In July 2002 she needed to be dry docked for maintenance, but the lower Mersey dry docks at Liverpool and Birkenhead were in use. The only alternative was for her to cruise up the ship canal to Trafford Wharf and use the dry docks still located there. The giant catamaran fitted into the locks with inches to spare, but managed to cruise the length of the canal without incident.

The MSC itself is undergoing a period of change as well. In the past, leisure craft were not allowed to cruise along the canal. Now, it is not unusual to see the occasional leisure narrowboat being allowed to use the canal for access to the river Weaver at Frodsham, the Shropshire Union Canal at Ellesmere Port, or for access to the river Mersey estuary at Eastham. The latter usually takes place during the Mersey River Festival when craft cruise across the Mersey (weather permitting) to the Albert Dock complex close to Liverpool's Pier Head. Although, with the planned Albert Dock link from the end of the Leeds and Liverpool Canal passing between the Pier Head and the Liver Building, this crossing of the Mersey from the ship canal will not be frequented by as many narrowboats and craft in the future.

Early in 2004 it was announced that there is a good possibility of the Runcorn Locks being reinstated. This is dependent upon a planned redevelopment of the area being successful and the construction of the proposed Mersey Second Crossing allowing approach roads to the existing suspension bridge to be relocated. A rally supporting the reinstatement of the locks took place in July 2004. If the plans come about the locks will connect to the MSC adjacent to Bridgewater House, allowing direct access to the Weaver Navigation via the MSC without the need to negotiate the Anderton Boat Lift.

In recent years, even with the slowing down of commercial traffic on the upper reaches of the MSC, there is still an annual tonnage of around 8 million tons of freight, with over 3,000 annual shipping movements. Peel Holdings (owners of the MSC) have recently announced that they plan to construct a new container terminal near Barton.

This new wharf will load vessels that will 'feed' larger ships moored at the deepwater container berth proposed for Liverpool's North Docks at Seaforth. This is a long-term project and may not come to fruition until around 2010, but will assure a continuing future for commercial trade on the MSC.

Looking down the new line of locks on the Bridgewater Canal at Runcorn, towards the MSC.

An aerial view of Wigg Wharf, Runcorn, once the unloading berth for the Guinness tankers from Ireland. This undated photograph, probably from the 1920s, shows a factory complex that occupied the site of the mustard gas production plant earlier in the century. The line of the Old Runcorn and Latchford Canal can be seen behind the factory complex.

Above: *Crossfields Transporter Bridge across the tidal Mersey near Warrington in 2003.*

Left: *The car that transports passengers and cargo across the river.*

Above: 'Dock Office' – the headquarters of
the Manchester Ship Canal Co. on Trafford
Road, Manchester.

Right: *An unusual photograph of Barton
Swing Aqueduct being swung, complete with
barge, c.1910. Note the horse on the
cantilevered towpath attached to the side of the
aqueduct.*

AD184	Fosse constructed at Castlefield by the Romans.
1697	Thomas Patten makes improvements to the river Mersey up to Warrington.
1712	Thomas Steers surveys the rivers Mersey and Irwell and suggests improvements to allow continuous navigation to Manchester.
1714	Mersey and Irwell Navigation Co. formed.
1734	Mersey and Irwell Navigation completed.
1737	Scroop Egerton commissions Thomas Steers to investigate making Worsley Brook and mine soughs navigable.
1754	Survey to make Sankey Brook navigable by Henry Berry.
1757	Sankey or Saint Helens Canal partially open.
1759	First Bridgewater Canal Act of Parliament.
1 July 1759	Construction commences on Bridgewater Canal.
17 July 1761	Act of Parliament for Barton Aqueduct is passed
1763	Connection made between Mersey and Irwell Navigation and Bridgewater Canal at Cornbrook ('the Gut').
21 March 1776	Bridgewater Canal opens to through traffic.
1804	Runcorn and Latchford Canal opens.
1821	Woolston New Cut is constructed.
1825	Proposal for ship canal from Runcorn to West Kirby is promoted and surveys by Thomas Telford are dropped, mainly due to cost.
1832	St Helens Canal extension to Widnes is constructed to counteract railway competition.
1838	Bridgewater Canal's Hulme Lock branch is built, superseding the previous connection to the river Irwell, 'the Gut'.
17 January 1846	Act of Parliament allowing the Bridgewater Canal to purchase the shares of the Mersey and Irwell Navigation, and the formation of the Bridgewater Navigation Co. Ltd.
1876	Upper Mersey Navigation Commission is established to light and buoy navigable channels to Bank Quay, Warrington, using the *Jesse Wallwork* as a tender, buoy lighter and survey vessel.
1877	Proposal by Hamilton Fulton for a ship canal to connect Manchester to the river Mersey estuary.
1882	Fulton's scheme for the MSC is adopted by Daniel Adamson and proposed to a group of Manchester businessmen, financiers and local mayors.
6 March 1883	MSC Bill passed by House of Commons but thrown out by the House of Lords on 9 August 1883.

In this 1960s aerial photograph, two tugs manoeuvre a ship past Barton Aqueduct and Bridge. In between the Bridgewater Canal and Barton Bridge Road on the left of the ship canal can be seen the embankment that led to Brindley's Aqueduct.

Narrowboats crossing Barton Swing Aqueduct with – judging by the style of dress – 1920s gongoozlers watching proceedings.

The ferryboat Pomona *and another unidentified craft moored at Albert Bridge, now the location of the Mark Addy public house, around the start of the twentieth century.*

November 1883	Ferdinand de Lesseps (engineer of the Suez Canal) visits Manchester to inspect plans for the MSC and asks to be kept informed of progress.
24 May 1884	MSC Bill is passed by the House of Lords, but thrown out by the House of Commons on 1 August 1884.
6 August 1885	Manchester Ship Canal Co. is formed and the MSC Bill is finally passed by both Houses of Parliament.
3 October 1885	Bridgewater Navigation Co. Ltd is purchased by Manchester Ship Canal Co. and a public holiday is declared in Manchester to celebrate the passing of the MSC Act of Parliament.
1886	Act of Parliament is passed to pay interest out of capital in order to raise £8 million on the stock exchange.

1887	Jubilee Exhibition contains scale model of MSC.
11 November 1887	Lord Egerton cuts the first sod of earth in the construction of the MSC at the site of the entrance locks at Eastham on the Wirral.
1888	Construction of MSC commences in eight sections: 1.) Eastham to Ellesmere Port; 2.) Ellesmere Port to Ince; 3.) Ince to Weston Point; 4.) Weston Point to Norton; 5.) Norton to Latchford; 6.) Latchford to Warburton; 7.) Warburton to Barton; and 8.) Barton to Manchester.
January 1889	Daniel Adamson dies at the age of seventy-one. Prolonged rain causes floods in fields and villages due to raised river levels. Temporary dams are washed away.
26 January 1889	Floods in Latchford section between Thelwall and Lymm wash machinery away and destroy embankments, leaving the railway lines suspended in mid-air. Between Little Bolton Cutting and Mode Wheel a barrier gives way, causing 20 million gallons of water to flood into the works in 20 minutes. In Trafford Cutting an ancient Runic Cross is discovered and a dugout canoe is also discovered at Partington. The railway locomotives *Rhymney* and *Deal* collide head-on, killing three workmen.
April 1889	Mersey Docks and Harbour Co. serve injunction against MSC for deviating from plans regarding openings in embankments which, allegedly, would alter the river Mersey's scouring affect, leading to damaging the river channel at Liverpool. Greenhart timber from British Guiana is delivered to Eastham for construction of the 80ft lock gates, which weigh 540 tons between them.
July 1889	Shah of Persia visits Manchester and wishes to see MSC workings. The remains of a dugout canoe are discovered at Barton.
7 November 1889	More rain and gales cause river levels to rise and breach temporary embankments, which lead to 6 miles of the workings to flood.
23 November 1889	River Irwell overflows at Barton.
25 November 1889	Thomas Walker, the contractor, dies aged sixty-two, and legal problems concerning his estate affect working on the ship canal's construction.
November 1890 to January 1891	More weather problems affected construction and weather did not abate until January 1891.
4 February 1891	Industrial disputes over wages affect construction.
9 March 1891	Special committee meeting with Manchester Corporation to request financial assistance. The corporation agree to advance £3 million and subsequently promoted a Bill in Parliament empowering them to do so. At a public meeting, Salford

Corporation were forced by public pressure to contribute £1 million, but the decision was denied due to the inability of Salford Corporation to borrow that amount of money.

5 June 1891   3,000 men work around the clock to complete the Eastham section.

13 June 1891   Regular packet steamer from Liverpool fails to dock at Ellesmere Port for the first time in fifty-four years. A £300 per day penalty was imposed on the MSC Co. due to Ellesmere Port

At the other end of the canal, this aerial view of Eastham Locks is prior to the construction of the Queen Elizabeth II oil terminal. Note the now disused barge lock being filled. The second craft from the left in the centre of the photograph is one of the paddle tugs used on the canal. Compare this photograph with the one at the beginning of Chapter Two.

	Docks and the Shropshire Union Canal basins being inaccessible from the river Mersey.
14 June 1891	Work commences to close the gap in the embankment using concrete. Tugs and dredgers moor in the river adjacent to the gap to act as breakwaters, protecting the embankment from tidal damage.
18 June 1891	Construction machinery is removed on completion of the Ellesmere Port section prior to filling. The actual date of filling this section of the canal was kept secret in order to prevent crowds from forming. A hole in the embankment was made and, as the tide rose, water slowly entered the canal. Filling of the section took over a week and, when it was completed, the only damage was minor landslips. However, when the hole in the embankment was filled-in on 11 July, the embankment was breached. The following day the breach was repaired with boulders but failed once again. It is eventually sealed with concrete and no further problems occur.
11 July 1891	River water entrance hole in embankment filled-in with soil.
12 July 1891	Embankment at Ellesmere Port is breached by tidal action and repaired using boulders, but is breached again.
13 July 1891	Breach is successfully repaired using concrete.
14 July 1891	The first passage along the ship canal from Eastham to Ellesmere Port takes place at 8.45 a.m. All subsequent traffic to Ellesmere Port had to go via the Ship Canal from Eastham.
1 August 1891	river Irwell is channelled into Little Barton Cutting.
14 September 1891	Ince section is filled without drama.
December 1891	Another financial crisis strikes. £863,000 is needed to complete the canal.
14 December 1891	Continuous rain causes the rivers Mersey and Irwell to breach embankments and flow into Irwell Cutting. At Latchford, the Bollin also bursts into the canal, causing damage and demolishing machinery. It is not a bad as the previous year – 2½ miles flooded as against 18½ miles.
1892	Amount required to complete the canal is raised to £1¼ million due to winter flood damage.
7 September 1892	Amount required to complete the canal is raised, yet again, to £2 million. Manchester Corporation raises rates to pay the amount. There is industrial unrest among workers. Irlam Railway Viaduct is tested by ten railway locomotives weighing a total of 750 tons.
29 May 1893	Barton Aqueduct is completed but a breach in approach to the aqueduct postpones demolition of Brindley's original aqueduct. When the breach was repaired, the Bridgewater Canal could be diverted over the new aqueduct and demolition

	of original aqueduct could take place. When this was achieved, this section of the canal was complete.
25 November 1893	Heavy rain causes both the Mersey and Irwell to flood into the completed, but partially filled, Runcorn and Latchford section. Within a week, the section was completed and the *Falmouth Castle* was the first ship to sail along it. This section was the last to be finished and construction work on the canal was completed from one end to the other.
21 December 1893	Manchester is declared a port for customs purposes.
30 December 1893	Chairman of Salford Quarter Sessions issues a certificate declaring that Manchester Docks are completed and ready to accept vessels.
31 December 1893	Manchester streets are crowded with people welcoming in the New Year and celebrating the impending opening of the canal.
1 January 1894	MSC is completed, and cost £14,347,891 to construct. At 10.00 a.m. a flotilla of ships headed by the steam yacht *Norsemen* leaves Eastham, and heads along the canal followed by the Wallasey ferryboats *Snowdrop* and *Crocus*. The first cargo carried along the whole length of the canal and discharged at Manchester was from the Co-operative Wholesale Societies' ship SS *Pioneer*.
21 May 1894	MSC is officially opened by Queen Victoria aboard the yacht *Enchantress*.
March 1895	Cotton trade between southern states of America and Manchester commences.
1898	Manchester Liners formed as a direct result of the cotton trade's success.
1899	A large flour mill constructed at Ellesmere Port is connected to the canal by the Mill Arm.
27 July 1901	*Chickahomony* brought the first bananas, mangos, oranges, rum, coconuts and logwood. Immediately after this, a two-way service started between the Caribbean and Manchester.
1902	First transporter bridge is constructed at Crossfields chemical plant, Warrington, to transport railway trucks across the river Mersey.
1905	New dock ½ mile-long is constructed on the site of the old racecourse and opened by King Edward VII, and the Runcorn–Widnes Transporter Bridge is completed.
1909	Water levels are raised throughout the whole length of the canal to give a maximum depth of 28ft.
1912	Transporter bridge at Crossfields plant in Warrington is constructed to carry railway trucks across the M&I Navigation. Elders & Fyffe's banana trade moved from Manchester to Liverpool Garston Docks.

1916	Excavation work commences at Stanlow Island for the first oil tanker berth, and Trafford Park industrial estate is founded close to Manchester Docks.
1922	Stanlow Island tanker berth is completed.
1927	Ship canal is deepened to 30ft between Eastham and Stanlow to accommodate 15,000 tons capacity oil tankers.
1933	Second (and larger) Stanlow Island tanker berth is completed adjacent to the first.
1940e	A ship carrying a whale oil cargo sheds its cargo into Manchester Docks, covering the water with a crust of emulsified oil. Boats clear the spillage, working like icebreakers, and the workers are paid £8 per day to clear the spillage.
1952	Construction work commences on Queen Elizabeth II oil terminal at Eastham which will cover 19 acres when completed.
January 1954	Opening of Queen Elizabeth II oil terminal, capable of handling ships of 35,000 tons and expansion of cargo-handling facilities for Colgate–Palmolive at Pomona Docks.
1960	Construction of Barton High-Level Bridge carrying the M602 motorway.
1966	Bridgewater Canal's new line of locks, part of Runcorn Docks, and the Runcorn and Weston Canal, are in-filled.
1970	New container berth is constructed at North Quay, Ellesmere Port
1972	All Liverpool Docks upstream of the Pier Head are closed except for Garston Docks.
1973	MSC Railway closes and the track subsequently removed except for that located within Trafford Park.
1974	Boat Museum established Ellesmere Port Docks at the Shropshire Union Canal's terminus and oil traffic from Bromborough to Crossfields at Warrington ceases.
1984	Bridgewater Estates and, shortly afterwards the Manchester Ship Canal, was purchased by Peel Holdings.
1985	Peel Holdings commence redevelopment of Manchester Docklands, starting with the Salford Quays complex on No.9 Dock.
1987	Cawoods container service to Manchester doubled and container handling facilities increased accordingly.
1988	Trafford Railway Swing Bridge is relocated to No.9 Dock where it was renamed Detroit Bridge.
1994	MSC's 100th anniversary celebrated by a commemorative boat rally held at Salford Quays.
1995	New Pomona Lock replaces Hulme Lock as the connection with the river Irwell and Manchester Docks, and there is the opening of new vertical lift bridge, the Centenary Bridge at Trafford Park close to Cerestar Wharf.

The view from the entrance locks at Eastham looking towards Liverpool in 1990. The scaffolding structures are called 'Dolphins' and are used to guide craft into the locks.

1996	Centenary Walk, a promenade along what is to be the Lowry Centre, is completed.
2000	Lowry Centre opens on North Bay (formally No. 9 Dock) and a dolphin is sighted in the lower reaches of the ship canal at Eastham.
2001	Proposal to utilise Pomona Dock as a marina to provide additional moorings for pleasure craft and the refurbishment of Weaste Wharf for trans-shipment of cement products.
July 2002	Imperial War Museum North, located at Trafford Wharf, opens to the public; *Super Seacat* cruises up the MSC to be dry docked at Trafford Wharf, and HMS *Bronnington* moves to the Historic Warships Collection at Wallasey Docks.
2003	Peel Holdings restructured into four divisions, one of which is Peel Ports who own the MSC, the Bridgewater Canal and the Mersey Docks and Harbour Company.
March 2004	Proposals unveiled for a new container terminal in the Barton area to load and unload feederships for the proposed deepwater container berth at Seaforth on the River Mersey Estuary opposite New Brighton.
November 2006	40 per cent of Peel Ports (of which the MSC is part) sold to the German Deutsche Bank, the Bridgewater Canal is unaffected.
July 2007	The BBC anounces the development of a Media City opposite the Lowry Centre at Salford Quays.
18 October 2007	Tesco commenced transporting wine from Liverpool Docks to their bottling and distribution facility at Irlam near Manchester by using container barges pushed by the tugs 'Daisy Doardo' and 'Res V'.

This 1966 photograph shows the QE2 Oil Berth and MSC approach locks. Wirral Metropolitan College's Carlett park campus is on the top right (the author's place of work).

Part of the QE2 Oil Berth and entrance lorks.

The large expanse of the QE2 Oil Berth at Eastham is illustrated by this photograph.

The Geography
of the Canal

Before entry onto the ship canal is attempted, permission must be obtained from the Manchester Ship Canal Co. For details of how to go about this, and what preparations need to be made before cruising the ship canal, please refer to the chapter on Navigational Information.

The northern end of the MSC is approached from the tidal river Mersey estuary at Eastham, upstream of the old Eastham ferry landing stage (now demolished). The river's channel is regularly dredged and is deceptively deep at this point. Navigation of the river Mersey should only be attempted while accompanied by a river Mersey Pilot and permission from the MSC must be obtained well in advance when access to the canal is required.

On arrival at the canal, there are four entrance locks. On the left are the old barge locks used by the Mersey flats and other barges small enough to fit. Use of these locks meant that a large amount of water was not wasted by barges using the larger ship locks. Adjacent to the barge locks are two sets of ship locks allowing passage to ships of larger dimensions. These locks have intermediate gates so that smaller craft do not have to use the full length of the locks, and in doing so, saving water. The fourth set of locks, on the right, slightly downstream from the ship canal entrance locks, incidentally the largest, are not actually connected to the ship canal, but allow tankers access to the Queen Elizabeth II oil terminal adjacent to the canal.

Also adjacent to the entrance locks are control sluices and the de-masting berths used for removing ship's funnels and masts when they were too tall to fit beneath the fixed bridges on the canal. Some later ships were constructed either to conform to the ship canal's dimensions or were fitted with telescopic masts and funnels that made the de-masting berths redundant. Tugs and 'gig' boats (small craft used for bringing ropes ashore) still use this area as their berths while waiting for the ships that they are to guide along the canal.

After passing through the entrance locks, the canal follows the banks of the river Mersey, from which the canal is separated by a narrow strip of land known as Pool Hall Bay Embankment. Before long, a small river passes beneath the canal in a 'syphon' and runs across the mudflats exposed at low tide, and into the river. The syphon is a technique pioneered by James Brindley when improving the mine drainage at the Wet Earth Collieries near Bolton, and also at Castlefield in Manchester where the river Medlock was diverted beneath the Bridgewater Canal's basins. This technique is used at many locations along the canal where a watercourse is required to cross the canal, but not to physically connect with it.

The rural setting of the canal's surroundings start to change to a more industrial nature and it is not long before Mount Manisty is reached. This is an artificial mound

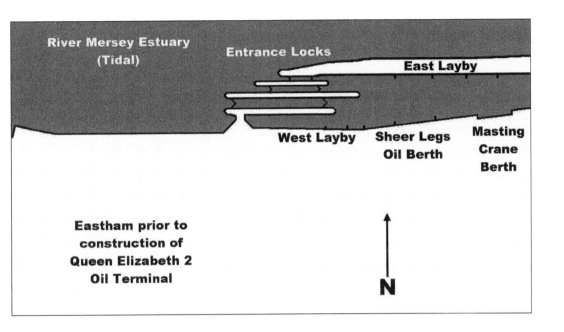

River Mersey Estuary (Tidal)

Entrance Locks

East Layby

West Layby

Sheer Legs Oil Berth

Masting Crane Berth

Eastham prior to construction of Queen Elizabeth 2 Oil Terminal

N

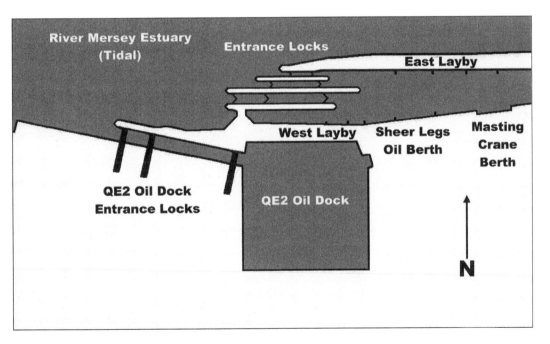

River Mersey Estuary (Tidal)

Entrance Locks

East Layby

West Layby

Sheer Legs Oil Berth

Masting Crane Berth

QE2 Oil Dock Entrance Locks

QE2 Oil Dock

N

Texaco tanker Texaco Bogata *and tug* Alfred *entering the QE2 Oil Dock at Eastham.*

Eastham Locks, looking towards Mount Manisty.

Eastham Locks, May 2005.

De-masting berth at Eastham, May 2005.

created by the waste from the canal's construction and named after the engineer in charge of the construction of this section of the canal. On the eastern bank can be seen the unloading berths for Bowater's Paper Mills, with the Vauxhall Motors' Ellesmere Port plant behind it. Mount Manisty is now a nature reserve and is home to many species of wildlife such as badgers, rabbits, hedgehogs and foxes, as is most of the embankment separating the canal from the river Mersey.

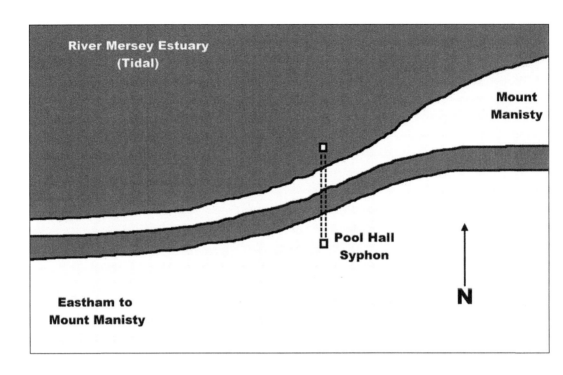

River Mersey Estuary
(Tidal)

Mount
Manisty

Pool Hall
Syphon

N

Eastham to
Mount Manisty

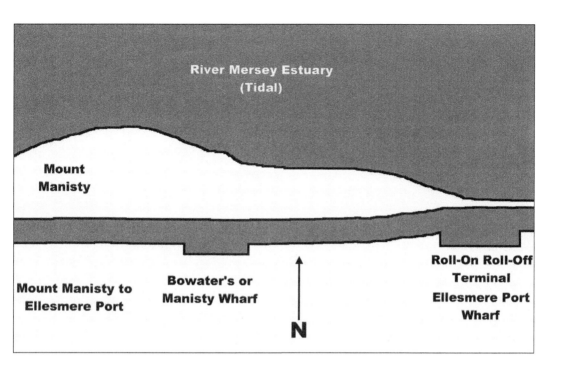

River Mersey Estuary
(Tidal)

Mount
Manisty

Mount Manisty to
Ellesmere Port

Bowater's or
Manisty Wharf

N

Roll-On Roll-Off
Terminal
Ellesmere Port
Wharf

Above: *View from Mount Manisty.*

Opposite below: *One of the navigation beacons that line the length of the canal. This particular example is marked '2' and is close to Mount Manisty.*

Shropshire Union Canal entrance basin looking towards Telford's Lighthouse and the MSC.

Shropshire Union Canal lower basin entrance lock.

Ellesmere Port Docks with Mount Manisty in the distance.

Looking towards Stanlow from the Shropshire Union Canal entrance locks.

The following four photographs show the lower basins of the Shropshire Union Canal at Ellesmere Port.

The next three photographs illustrate the narrow and broad locks at the start of the Shropshire Union Canal and the location of the Boat Museum.

Above: *Boat Museum Entrance Locks and Telford's Lighthouse.*

The outfall of Pool Hall syphon near Mount Manisty.

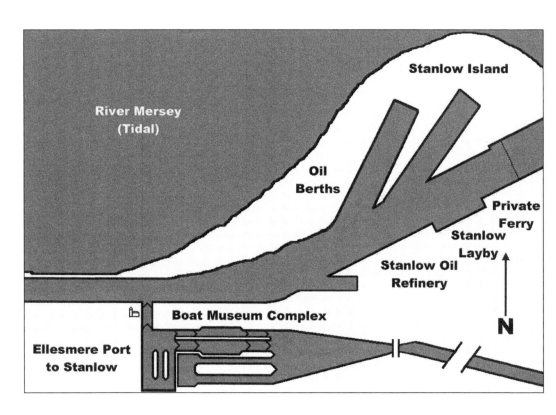

Solon, *unloading at Ellesmere Port in 1993.*

Telford's Lighthouse, prior to restoration, which originally marked the entrance locks to the Shropshire Union Canal at Ellesmere Port. Since the construction of the MSC, it has been one of the few lighthouses on the inland waterways system.

The Boat Museum's lower basin. In the distance the ex-MSC tug Daniel Adamson *is moored. Recently, the future of this craft has been uncertain, but a preservation society has been formed to ensure its conservation.*

A concrete barge moored in the lower basin close to the location of the warehouses that were destroyed by fire in May 1970.

About a mile on from Bowater's Wharf is the Ellesmere Port container terminal, built in 1970 on the North Quay. RoRo car ferries bring in foreign cars as well as taking British cars for export and container ships from all over the world. It is not uncommon to see Russian, Spanish and Japanese ships moored next to each other at the quay. Adjacent to the container terminal is the entrance to the Shropshire Union Canal and its numerous basins. Thomas Telford's original lighthouse stands sentinel over the entrance locks and dates from 1828 when, prior to the construction of the ship canal, the canal ran straight into the Mersey estuary. Today it has the distinction of being the only lighthouse on the British inland waterways system.

There were extensive warehouses located here, the most famous being 'Telford's Warehouses' constructed to house clay for the potteries and other commodities not suitable for storage outside. Their graceful arches spanned the basins until they were damaged by fire in May 1970, and had to be demolished. Today the area is home to the Boat Museum, one of the premier museums of canal and inland navigation history in the country.

The museum has a wide range of craft and exhibits on display, ranging from the *Mersey Flats*, a concrete barge; narrowboats; various historic canal craft; and even a 'starvationer' as used inside the Worsley Mines on the Bridgewater Canal. There is a café and a large shop selling canalia, books, videos and so on. The museum is well worth a visit and can provide a special plaque for visitors arriving by boat, regardless of which canal they arrive on. Arrangements can be made to moor in the museum's basins over night and while visiting the museum. It is also one of the few 'bolt holes' for small (by ship canal standards) craft traversing the ship canal.

Opposite the Boat Museum, the embankment separating the ship canal from the river Mersey gives way to a concrete dam, which is where water was first admitted into this section of the canal and caused so many problems in November 1892.

The Boat Museum is followed by the Stanlow Oil Refinery and its tanker berths. These berths, constructed in 1922 and 1933, are located on Stanlow Island. The island was once home to Stanlow Priory where Benedictine or 'Black' monks lived until the priory was closed. The monks petitioned the Pope for a licence to relocate the priory to a new site at Whalley, close to Blackburn in Lancashire, permission for which was eventually granted. The reason for the closure of the priory was the encroachment of the river, and the severe weather that constantly battered the buildings during the winter, conditions that were also prevalent during the construction of the canal. Today, the remains of the priory buildings can still be traced in the undergrowth. The only residents on the island are rabbits, hares, badgers, foxes and other wildlife. The older buildings on the island still bear the camouflage that disguised them from the probing eyes of the Luftwaffe during the Second World War.

It is only possible to reach Stanlow Island by ferryboat from the refinery opposite, although, when researching and photographing the canal, I did walk from Eastham to Stanlow along the embankment that separates the canal from the river, a practice that is not encouraged by the Manchester Ship Canal or Shell UK which controls the oil berths at Stanlow. There are two berths located on the island plus a turning basin, used when manoeuvring tankers in and out of the berths. The Stanlow Island Ferry runs from one of the lay-bys on the canal, opposite the island. Ships can moor in the lay-by

A barge coming around the turn at Ellesmere Port, heading towards Eastham in 1985.

Looking across the MSC to Stanlow Island.

The private ferry at Stanlow Island connecting the island to the refinery in 1990.

to await access to the main oil berths on the island or load and unload if access to the main berths is not required. The hose-handling rigs installed here rise and fall with the ships as their cargo is discharged or loaded.

On the southern side of the island, the river Gowy passes beneath the ship canal in a syphon. At one time, the point were the Gowy runs into the Mersey was used for mooring craft and a tide refuge can still be seen poking out of the mud. The river Gowy forms the southern geographical boundary of the Wirral Peninsula, and the ship canal now enters Cheshire as it passes along the side of the oil refinery with its numerous berths and lay-bys. The refinery is followed by Ince Power Station, which possesses unloading wharves. At one time, the power station received fuel in the form of shale oil delivered via the ship canal and unloaded at the wharf.

The flat marshlands that follow Stanlow are the Ince and Frodsham marshes. They indicate the edge of the Cheshire Plain, created after the Ice Age, when the glaciers melted and their waters ran to the sea, forming the Mersey Basin in the process. Due to the marshes being only slightly above sea level, they are criss-crossed by many drainage dykes or gutters, which come together and pass beneath the ship canal in a syphon before running into the Mersey at Frodsham Score. The towns of Frodsham and Helsby can be seen in the distance huddling beneath the stone outcrops of the hills that protect them. If Helsby Hill is viewed from the south, at a particular angle, the profile of a Native American's face can be seen in the rock-face.

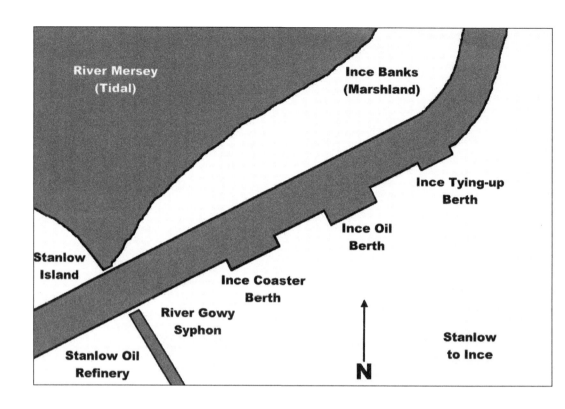

Two tankers discharging their cargo at Stanlow Island in 1989.

The Stanlow Island ferry-landing stage looking towards Ince.

An old disused marker beacon on Stanlow Island.

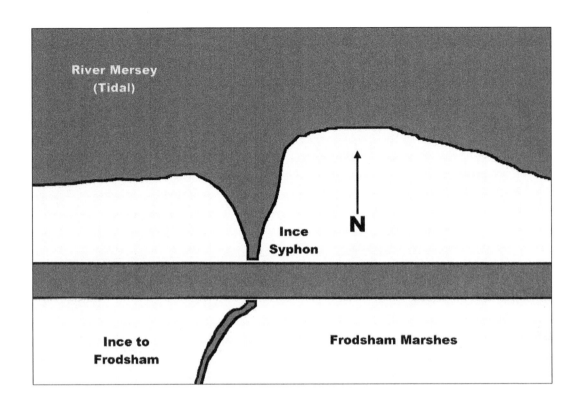

River Mersey
(Tidal)

N

Ince
Syphon

Ince to
Frodsham

Frodsham Marshes

The river Gowy as it passes through Stanlow Oil Refinery.

Stanlow Oil Refinery from Stanlow Island with the river Gowy syphon in the foreground.

A tidal refuge at Stanlow Island.

The mouth of the river Weaver at its junction with the MSC at Weston Marsh Lock.

Weston Marsh Lock, which connects the MSC with the Weaver Navigation and the Runcorn and Weston Canal. ICI's Castner Kellner chemical plant is in the background.

Looking towards Weston Point from Weston Marsh Lock with the Weaver Sluices, which control excess water from the river Weaver, in the background.

The disused part of Runcorn Docks in 1987, now in-filled. Hopefully it will be re-opened, along with the new line of locks connecting the Runcorn Arm of the Bridgewater Canal with the Runcorn and Weston Canal.

Runcorn Docks during the late 1980s, situated in the centre of the chemical industry.

Bridgewater House, looking isolated in 1987. Today the building is used as a college.

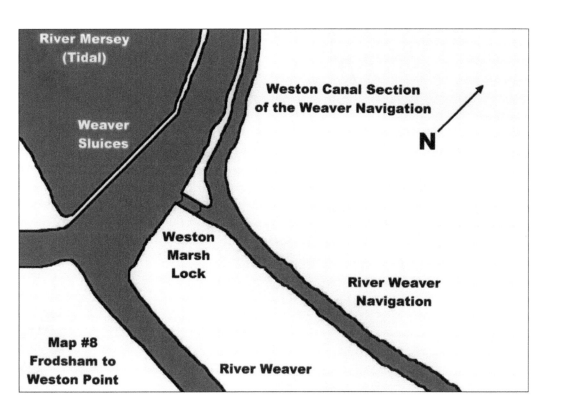

Map #8
Frodsham to
Weston Point

Bridgewater House, Runcorn.

Above and opposite: *Two views from either side of the Runcorn Bridge in 1986.*

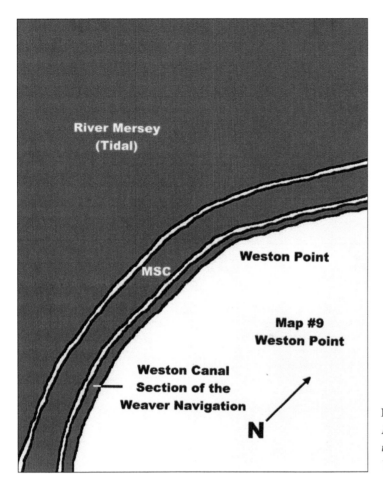

River Mersey (Tidal)

Weston Point

MSC

Map #9 Weston Point

Weston Canal Section of the Weaver Navigation

N

Below: *The ship canal and Mersey estuary, looking towards Eastham from Weston Point.*

The MSC tug Talisman at Old Quay. Note the telescopic masts on the ship in the background.

The span of the Runcorn Widnes Bridge is illustrated in this photograph. At one time it was the longest single-span catilever bridge in Europe.

Frodsham Marshes at this point contain sludge ponds where dredgings from the ship canal are deposited. The canal clings to the river Mersey's banks as it starts a giant 's' bend, lasting until Runcorn.

The first sweeping curve towards Weston Point, before which, the river Weaver runs across the canal. Soon, the ship canal widens out as the entrance to the river Weaver is reached. The water running down the river Weaver feeds into the ship canal and, opposite the river's mouth are situated sluices through which the river's water empties into the river Mersey. Care must be exercised due to the volume of water passing across the canal after periods of rain. Shortly after the entrance to the river Weaver can be seen Weston Marsh Lock, the entrance lock to the Weaver Navigation. This is a canal that bypasses the lower section of the river Weaver, and the location was named 'Salt Port' due to the primary substance that was loaded into ships at this point. Today, it is the location of the giant ICI Castner Kellner chemical plant. At night, when illuminated, this complex is especially impressive. The Weaver Navigation also gave access to the Trent and Mersey Canal via the restored Anderton Boat Lift and the disused Runcorn and Weston Canal that originally connected to Runcorn Docks and the Bridgewater Canal.

As the ship canal rounds the bend created by Weston Point there are three waterways side by side: the river Mersey, the Manchester Ship Canal and the Runcorn and Weston Canal. Just before Runcorn Docks are reached the disused Weston Mersey Lock is visible, which gave flats and barges access to the river at that point. Shortly after this, the Runcorn and Weston Canal reaches its destination, leaving the Mersey and the ship canal to their own devices.

Once around the bend at Weston Point, the canal passes the disused entrance locks that gave access from the ship canal to the Bridgewater Canal. The locks, now sadly filled-in, are watched over by Bridgewater House, an impressive mansion built by Francis Egerton for James Brindley and himself to live in while overseeing the construction of their canal. The house dates from a period of time when a window tax was imposed. Consequently, many of what appear to be windows are actually imitations painted onto the brickwork. Today, the house is part of Halton Community College. Another wharf at Runcorn is Wigg Wharf, made famous for the bulk handling of Guinness.

The adjacent river Mersey now narrows considerably and, consequently, the first bridge crossings of the river and the ship canal now loom in the distance. First is the Victoria Railway Bridge carrying the main railway line from Liverpool to London. This is quickly followed by the Runcorn–Widnes Silver Jubilee Bridge, constructed in 1964 to replace the earlier transporter bridge, opened in 1905, that occupied a location adjacent to today's bridge. Plans are being made for a second road bridge to supplement the first, as traffic volume has exceeded the levels that it was designed to carry. The new bridge will most probably be situated around 1 mile upstream from the first at Astmoor.

Above and below: *Two photographs in the vicinity of Old Quay Swing Bridge, Runcorn.*

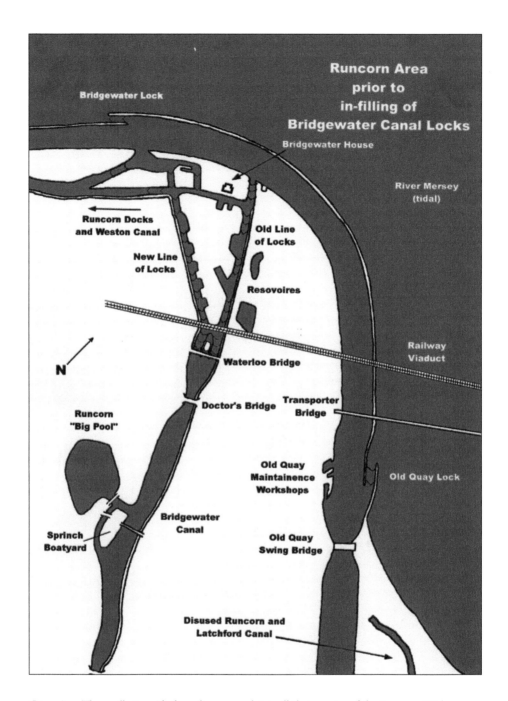

Opposite: *The small pier with the railings around it is all that remains of the Runcorn–Widnes Transporter Bridge.*

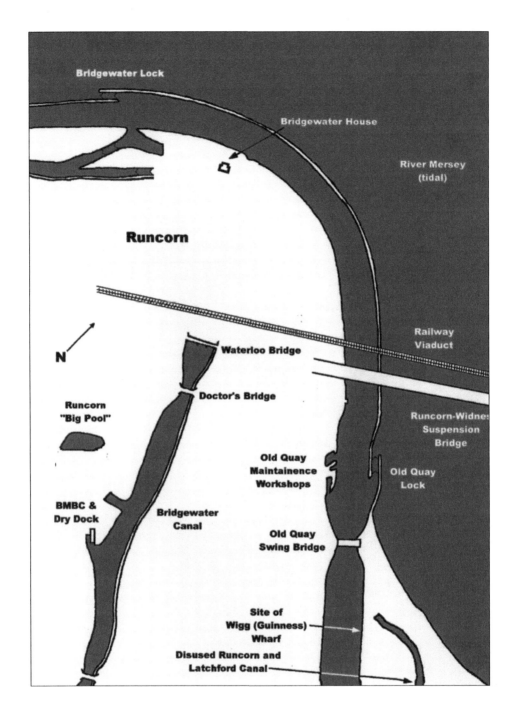

Opposite above: *A barge moored in the disused Old Quay Lock.*
Opposite below: *Spare lock gates stored opposite the Old Quay Workshops.*

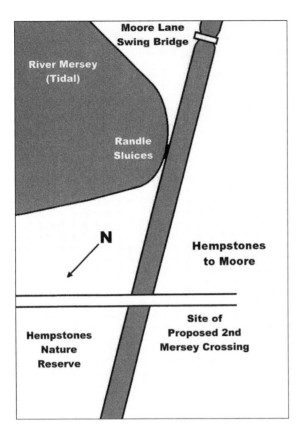

River Mersey
(Tidal)

Randle
Sluices

N

Hempstones
to Moore

Site of
Proposed 2nd
Mersey Crossing

Hempstones
Nature
Reserve

The two photographs below and opposite of Wigg Wharf, Runcorn, are separated by sixty years.

Below: *This illustrates the close proximity to the disused Runcorn and Latchford Canal.*

This photograph shows a Guinness tanker unloading 'black velvet' into road tankers to be transported to the bottling/canning/distribution plant.

After the suspension bridge is the disused Old Quay Lock, which used to give access to the upper reaches of the Mersey and Widnes Dock, the terminus of the St Helens Canal. Opposite the lock are the MSC's Old Quay workshops. This is the headquarters of the canal's Maintenance Department, and home to the dredgers that can sometimes be seen removing silt from the ship canal's bed. The first of the canal's swing bridges can now be seen in the distance. These bridges were designed by Edward Leader Williams, and bear a striking similarity to those on the river Weaver. This is not surprising really, as Leader Williams was the engineer of that waterway before moving to the ship canal.

On the marshlands just after the Old Quay Swing Bridge is the Hempstones Nature Reserve. This was the location of Wigg Wharf, where Guinness was imported from Ireland. Previous to this it was the site of a First World War mustard gas factory and, after the factory was demolished, the contaminated land was capped with concrete. Building on this land is not allowed due to possible contamination, but if the area is explored, the remains of the Runcorn and Latchford Canal can be seen. This was a canal opened in 1804, and was an extension to the old Mersey and Irwell Navigation. It linked Runcorn to Woolston Cut without the risks and unpredictability of having to navigate the tidal river, and was a more direct route cutting off many meanders in the Mersey. The entrance lock from the Mersey has long since disappeared, although its location can still be seen in the mudflats. Parts of the canal have been swallowed up by the construction of the MSC but there are still many isolated remains to be seen, including some of the locks, one of which is located around a bend in the canal a short walk along its length. This area is also the location for the proposed Runcorn Widnes second crossing. This is to be a road bridge to supplement the original Runcorn Widnes bridge. The new bridge will also accommodate a light railway deck suspended below the roadway for trams.

Above and left: *Two computer-generated images of how the new bridge may look. Note the light railway/tramway slung beneath the main carriageway on the close-up of the bridge.*

The Mersey widens out after Runcorn Gap, and then narrows opposite Fiddler's Ferry Power Station, where it starts its characteristic meandering. The river continues its meandering westwards through the Crossfields Chemical Works at Bank Quay near Warrington, where it is crossed by the historic transporter bridge. Originally, there were two transporter bridges here. The first one was built in 1902 and carried railway trucks from one side of the river to the other and is now demolished. The second one, built in 1912, was recently bought by Warrington Council, and is now disused. However, it is a listed structure, is complete and is awaiting restoration.

After passing numerous industrial estates on the edge of Runcorn, the ship canal now leaves (temporarily) the company of the Mersey and enters a cutting. The Promenade caravan park is situated on the right-hand bank of the canal and soon Randles Sluices are reached. Here, excess water is run-off from the ship canal into a nearby meander of the Mersey. There is also a subway beneath the canal through which the Vyrnwy water pipeline passes. Just past Moore Lane lay-by is the Moore Lane Swing Bridge, followed by Acton Grange Wharf used by Dupont UK, and the Acton Grange Railway Viaduct. The next canal crossing is a railway viaduct followed by Chester Road Swing Bridge where the A5060 Chester Road is carried over the canal. This is followed by Warrington Wharf, Walton Cut and a sand berth. The lock at Walton Cut gave access to the river diversion and the section of the Mersey that runs alongside the A5060 Chester Road through to the centre of Warrington. The next swing bridge is Northwich Road Swing Bridge, which carries the A49 London Road. Adjacent to the bridge is the old Twenty Steps Lock where the Runcorn and Latchford Canal cut across yet another meandering section of the Mersey up to Woolston Cut and Woolston New Cut. These are canalised sections of the river which made up part of the Mersey and Irwell Navigation improvements during the eighteenth century.

On the eastern bank of the canal is Stockton Heath, and Latchford High-Level Bridge (similar in design to Warburton High-Level Bridge further along the canal) soon spans the canal. This high-level bridge is one of the few fixed bridges on the canal. The canal continues along a ruler-straight section in a deep cutting to Knutsford Road Swing Bridge where the A50 crosses the canal, followed by Latchford Railway Viaduct and Latchford.

Runcorn and Latchford Canal looking towards Fiddler's Ferry Power Station, 1987.

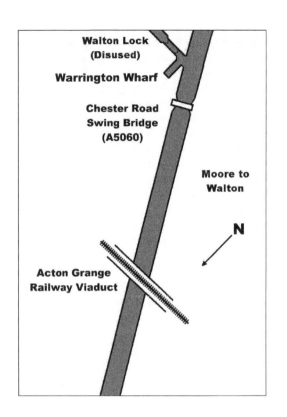

Walton Lock
(Disused)

Warrington Wharf

**Chester Road
Swing Bridge
(A5060)**

**Moore to
Walton**

N

**Acton Grange
Railway Viaduct**

The isolated Moore Lane Swing Bridge halfway between Runcorn and Stockton Heath.

Acton Grange Railway Viaduct.

Northwich Road Swing Bridge carries the A49 over the MSC at Stockton Heath.

Immediately after Northwich Road Swing Bridge is the in-filled remains of part of the Runcorn and Latchford Canal.

Above: *One of two virtually identical high-level bridges carrying minor roads across the canal. This example is Latchford High-Level Road Bridge, and the other is Warburton High-Level Bridge.*

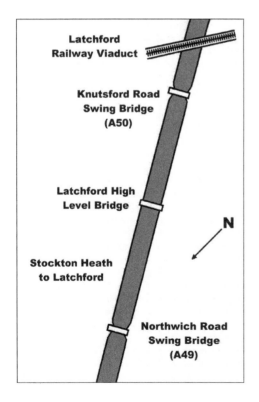

Above: *Chester Road Swing Bridge, seen from the canal when closed to road traffic.*

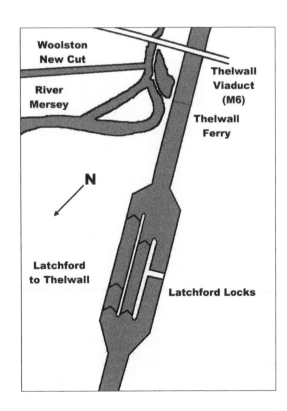

Opposite below, right: *Latchford Railway Viaduct.*

Latchford Locks in 2003, showing the New World domestic appliance factory on the offside of the canal.

Locks giving a rise of 42ft 6in. These locks are the first to be encountered since the entrance locks at Eastham, 21 miles distant. They are duplicated locks with intermediate gates in each chamber to keep water wastage on the canal to a minimum. Adjacent to the locks, on the left-hand bank, is the 'New World' domestic appliance factory, famous for cookers and other household appliances.

The Mersey meanders towards the canal on the left-hand bank, but there is no actual connection until a little further on at Rixton Junction. At Thelwall Ferry, a rowing boat is used to ferry pedestrians across the canal. The ferry only operates at certain times of the day, and an adjacent notice board gives details of the hours of operation. On the western bank, a little way past the ferry, is situated the Woolston Deposit Grounds, one of the locations where dredgings from the ship canal are dumped. Thelwall High-Level Bridge, better known as Thelwall Viaduct, carries the M6 motorway not only over the ship canal but the river Mersey as well. In recent years, the viaduct has undergone considerable work as the expansion rollers supporting the roadway were found to be crumbling. This necessitated the replacement of all the rollers, as well as other remedial work. The approach embankments span the Bridgewater Canal, a disused railway and the A56 trunk road. Statham golf course is on the right-hand bank of the ship canal and contains isolated meanders of the Mersey within its grounds. The Butcher's Field Cut of the river Mersey joins the ship canal on the left at Rixton Junction (also known as Bollin Point) where, on the opposite bank, the river Bollin also runs into the canal.

Right: *A rowing boat, still in use as a ferryboat, at Thelwall Ferry in 2003.*

Below: *The noticeboard at Thelwall Ferry.*

THELWALL FERRY
FROM 17th October 1982 By Agreement with
CHESHIRE COUNTY COUNCIL AND
WARRINGTON BOROUGH COUNCIL THE
FERRY WILL OPERATE BETWEEN THE
FOLLOWING HOURS :

	0700	to	0900
TOLL EACH WAY	1200	to	1400
CHILDREN	1600	to	1900

Except Sundays & Bank Holidays

The canal now bends to the right in the first proper bend since Runcorn. Warburton High-level Bridge carries the B5159 across the canal and is a toll bridge connecting the A6144 to the A57. A toll of 12p is charged (at the time of writing) for the passage of vehicles, not to cross the bridge over the ship canal, but to cross the remains of the original bridge that carried the road over the dry bed of the river Mersey, and later the Mersey and Irwell Navigation. Just after the bridge, a pipeline passes beneath the canal and a disused meander of the river Mersey, partly in water, joins the canal. The original line of the river is visible for quite a way across adjacent the fields if viewed from Warburton High-Level Bridge, and it is this original line of the river that was crossed by the toll bridge. After another bend, the canal was crossed by Bob's Ferry, now disused, which allowed a pedestrian connection between Partington and Cadishead.

Cadishead Viaduct takes a railway line across the ship canal. Immediately after this is the Partington North and South Wharves, both of which serve the chemical and petro-chemical plants nearby. After Irlam Wharf, on the right, is the Mersey Weir where the river runs into the canal from its source in the hills above Stockport. As is usual when a river runs into the canal, care must be exercised after rainfall, due to the high volume of water running into the canal which can push craft towards the opposite bank. Next to the weir is Irlam Railway Viaduct whose strength, after construction, was tested at the insistence of the railway company by driving ten railway locomotives onto it at the same time, which had a total weight of 750 tons. The test was successful and no modifications had to be made to it.

Warburton High-Level Bridge and approach embankments, seen from over the fields bordering the MSC.

Above: *The view from Warburton High-Level Bridge. The disused meander that led to the original Warburton Toll Bridge can be seen in the distance.*

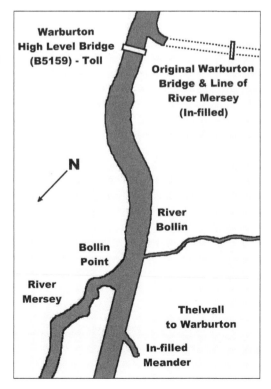

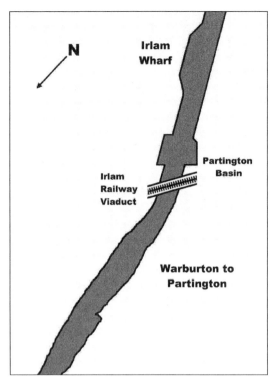

N

Irlam
Wharf

Partington
Basin

Irlam
Railway
Viaduct

Warburton to
Partington

Below: *A view of the canal looking towards Irlam.*

A lay-by precedes Irlam Locks, which give a rise of 16ft, and is followed by yet another lay-by. The original course of the river Irwell is to the left of the locks. After the locks, a long sweeping bend is punctuated by Hulme Bridge Ferry, Davyhulme Sludge Berths and Barton Locks, which give a rise of 15ft. There are lay-bys situated before and after the locks. Barton High-Level Bridge, as previously mentioned, originally carried the M62 Urmston Bypass, later to become the M63 and later still the M60.

Shortly after Barton High-Level Bridge is a control tower on an island in the centre of the canal. This is the location of Barton Road Bridge (B5211 – Barton/Redclyffe Road) and the famous Barton Swing Aqueduct (Bridgewater Canal). Both bridges are controlled by an operator situated in the adjacent control tower. The tower was staffed 24 hours a day in years gone by, when the ship canal was busier than it is now. Today, staff are only present when necessary.

The Swing Aqueduct replaced James Brindley's original aqueduct, which originally carried the Bridgewater Canal across the Mersey and Irwell Navigation. On construction of the ship canal, Brindley's original structure was not demolished until the swing aqueduct was completed and open to traffic, in order to maintain a continuous route for boats on the Bridgewater Canal, which was heavily used by commercial traffic at that time. The line of the original aqueduct can still be traced, as can the smaller aqueduct over Barton Lane and the location of the approach embankments.

The dredger MSC Ince. Dredging is a vital process to remove the silt brought into the canal from the rivers Mersey and Irwell.

A collection of vessels passing through Irlam Locks.

Looking towards Manchester from Barton Road Bridge in the 1960s. Note the aqueduct in the swung position.

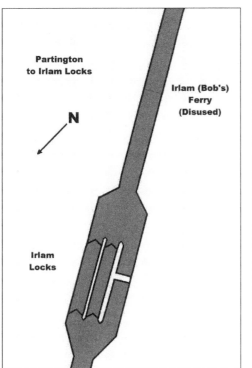

Partington
to Irlam Locks

Irlam (Bob's)
Ferry
(Disused)

N

Irlam
Locks

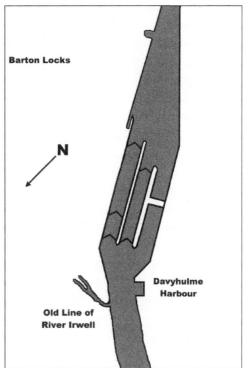

Barton Locks

N

Davyhulme
Harbour

Old Line of
River Irwell

An aerial view of Barton Road Bridge and Barton Swing Aqueduct. In this 1987
photograph the aqueduct is painted red and white. The colour scheme did not last long, and
soon reverted to the more usual grey and white.

Mason's mark, Barton Aqueduct.

The MSC tug Ulex *assists a cargo vessel past Barton Swing Aqueduct and Barton Road Bridge.*

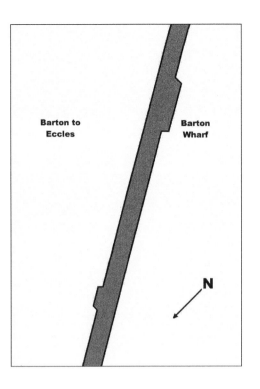

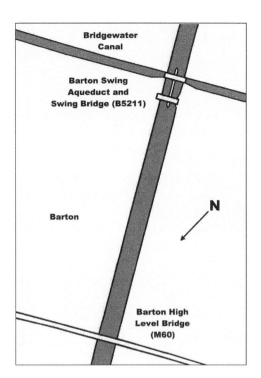

Barton to Eccles

Barton Wharf

N

Bridgewater Canal

Barton Swing Aqueduct and Swing Bridge (B5211)

Barton

N

Barton High Level Bridge (M60)

Centenary Lift Bridge.

The ship canal at Trafford Park, looking towards Barton.

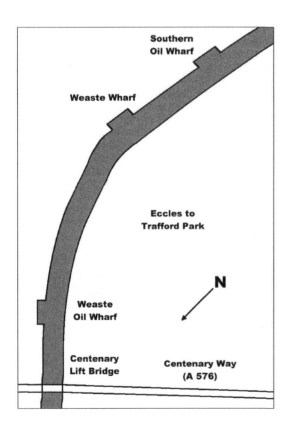

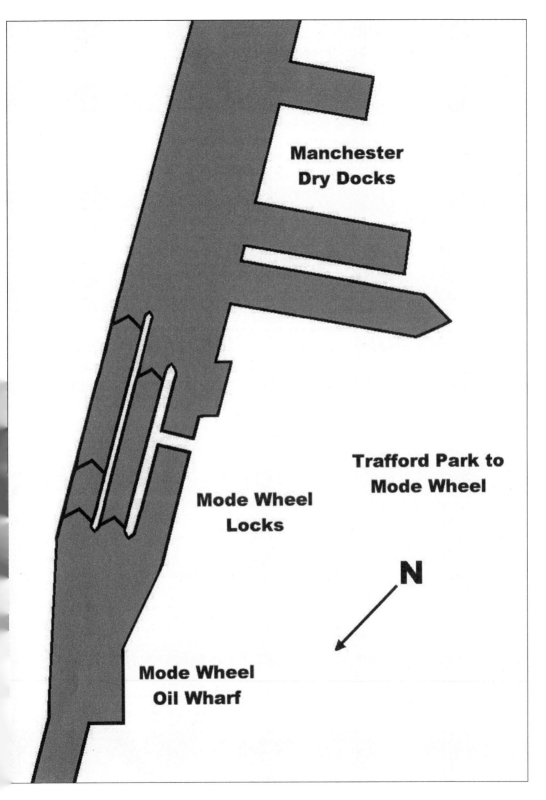

Manchester
Dry Docks

Trafford Park to
Mode Wheel

Mode Wheel
Locks

N

Mode Wheel
Oil Wharf

Over the years, the swing aqueduct itself has not escaped modification. At one time, in the late 1980s, it was painted red and white instead of the usual grey colour. At the time the repainting was done, the towpath that cantilevered over the water channel of the Bridgewater Canal was removed, as was the approach ramp on the Patricroft side.

As the ship canal approaches the outskirts of Manchester, there are numerous wharves and landing stages, some of which are now disused. One wharf that is still active is the Cerestar Wharf where various raw materials are unloaded and edible products loaded. This unusual bridge was opened in 1995 and has a span of 43m. It was the first movable bridge to be built on the canal since 1895, and carries Centenary Way (A576) across the canal just before it bends to the right at Little Bolton. More factories and wharves signal the approach to Mode Wheel Locks, the last on the canal. These locks give a rise of 13ft and complete the 60½ft-climb to Manchester Docks and the river Irwell summit level.

Immediately after the locks, on the right-hand bank, are the dry and graving docks owned by Manchester Dry Docks Ltd. Here, ships have had repairs made as well as being the final resting place of many that have reached the end of their lives to be dismantled and scrapped.

The MSC now reaches its ultimate destination of Manchester Docks. The once-busy docks have now been redeveloped into business and housing complexes. The first dock is now called the North Bay (previously No.9 Dock) and its banks are dominated by the Lowry Art Gallery, Lowry Shopping Centre and Salford Quays. Opposite is Trafford Wharf, the location of the Imperial War Museum North. The Millennium Lifting Footbridge spans the canal, connecting Trafford Wharf to the Lowry Centre for pedestrians, and marks the boundary separating the MSC from Manchester Docks. The bridge is a vertical lift bridge of similar design to the Centenary Bridge a little way downstream although, with commercial traffic no longer using this stretch of the canal, it is rarely lifted. Pleasure craft are not permitted to navigate below Lowry Footbridge without prior arrangements being made with the MSC Co. and craft are allowed to moor at various locations above Lowry Footbridge.

North Bay continues on to Huron and Erie Basins, the two basins being divided by the relocated Trafford Railway Swing Bridge, relocated from further upstream and converted into a fixed footbridge. A new canal, the Mariners' Canal, connects to Ontario Basin, a continuation of Central Bay, the next bay along. Central Bay is connected to Ontario Basin by the newly constructed Welland Canal and Lock. Adjacent to the lock are moorings conveniently located for visiting the Lowry Centre and Imperial War Museum North. Welland Lock connects to St Louis and St Peter Basins, access to which is currently strictly controlled, although it is planned to allow pleasure craft access through Welland Lock on the first weekend of the month during the summer period. Located in the base of Welland Lock's control tower is a sanitary station, water point and rubbish disposal, access to which is by the conventional BW key.

Looking downstream towards Mode Wheel Locks. Manchester Dry Docks are on the left-hand side.

HMS Bronington, *a minesweeper once commanded by HRH The Prince of Wales, is pictured here moored outside the Imperial War Museum North before it was moved to the Historic Warships Collection in Wallasey Docks.*

An undated photograph of No.5 Dock

The same location when Salford Quays was under construction in 1988.

Detroit Footbridge, the relocated Trafford Rail Swing Bridge between Huron and Erie Basins.

Millennium Footbridge connects the Lowry Complex to the Imperial War Museum North and Trafford Promenade.

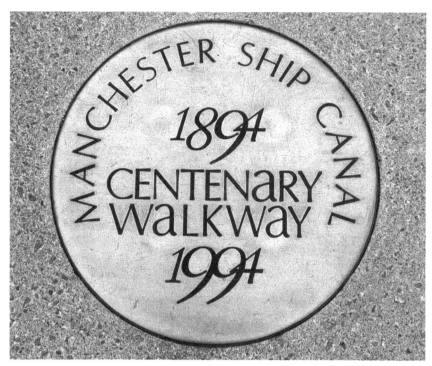

One of the commemorative plaques in the pavement of Centenary Walkway, Salford Quays.

Welland Lock gives access to Mariner's Canal, Ontario, Erie and Huron Basins.

Mariner's Canal connects Ontario Basin to Erie Basin.

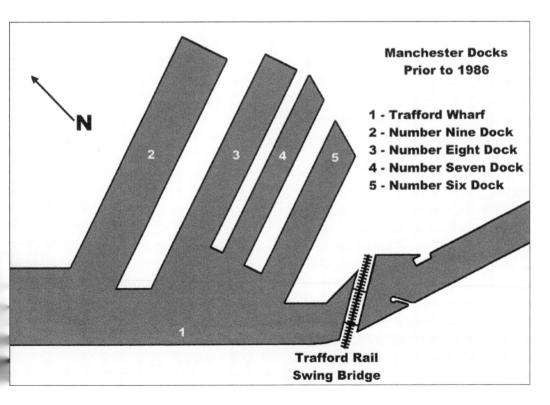

Above and below: *These two images of No.9 Dock/Salford Quays are separated by nearly forty years.*

Above: *Erie Basin.*
Below: *The Victoria Building is one of the architectural wonders of the Salford Quays.*

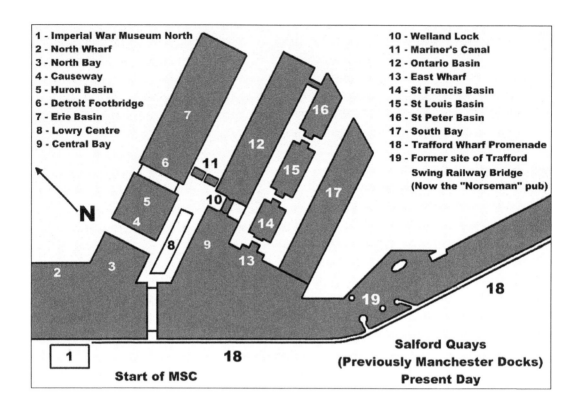

1 - Imperial War Museum North
2 - North Wharf
3 - North Bay
4 - Causeway
5 - Huron Basin
6 - Detroit Footbridge
7 - Erie Basin
8 - Lowry Centre
9 - Central Bay

10 - Welland Lock
11 - Mariner's Canal
12 - Ontario Basin
13 - East Wharf
14 - St Francis Basin
15 - St Louis Basin
16 - St Peter Basin
17 - South Bay
18 - Trafford Wharf Promenade
19 - Former site of Trafford
      Swing Railway Bridge
      (Now the "Norseman" pub)

Start of MSC

Salford Quays
(Previously Manchester Docks)
Present Day

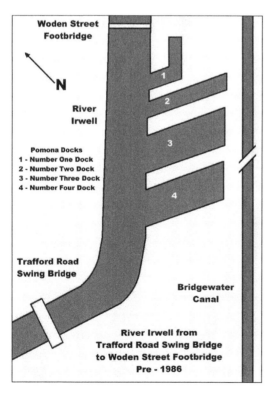

Woden Street
Footbridge

River
Irwell

Pomona Docks
1 - Number One Dock
2 - Number Two Dock
3 - Number Three Dock
4 - Number Four Dock

Trafford Road
Swing Bridge

Bridgewater
Canal

River Irwell from
Trafford Road Swing Bridge
to Woden Street Footbridge
Pre - 1986

Opposite above and below: *These two photographs of Trafford Turn are separated by 110 years. Pomona Nos 1-4 Docks are behind the photographer in both cases.*

Detroit Footbridge.

The Atlantic Fisher, *moored at Trafford Wharf in 1988, was one of the last ships of this size to use Manchester Docks before the area was redeveloped.*

Manchester container terminal served a weekly Manchester–Montreal cellular ship service for Manchester Liners.

Noticeboard at the junction of Pomona Dock and the river Irwell, 2003.

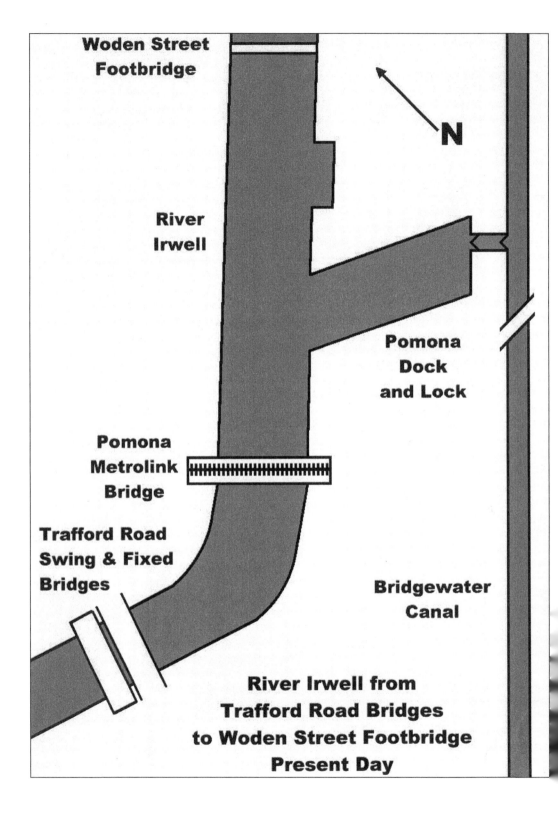

Woden Street
Footbridge

N

River
Irwell

Pomona
Dock
and Lock

Pomona
Metrolink
Bridge

Trafford Road
Swing & Fixed
Bridges

Bridgewater
Canal

River Irwell from
Trafford Road Bridges
to Woden Street Footbridge
Present Day

The author's narrowboat, Total Eclipse, *in Pomona Lock, May 2003.*

Two pleasure craft are passing Trafford Road Swing Bridge in 1988, prior to the construction of the fixed bridge alongside the swing bridge.

After Central Bay are East Wharf North and South and the South Bay. Immediately after South Bay was the original location of Trafford Railway Swing Bridge, which is now in North Bay. An unusually shaped basin on the left was where the bridge swung away from the bank of the canal, and some of the supports can still be seen as can the pivot island on the right, which is now built upon and is part of the Wharfside Promenade. Trafford Fixed and Swing Bridges follow. The swing bridge was once the largest of this type in England.

The next crossing, around a right-hand bend, is the Manchester Metrolink Bridge, below Pomona Dock, taking the city's tram system into the heart of the redeveloped docks area and beyond. The dock on the right is Pomona No.3 Dock, and is the location of a proposed marina complex. At the far end of the dock is Pomona Lock, which connects with the Bridgewater Canal. This lock was constructed in 1995 to replace Hulme Lock, about a mile further upstream. The sites of Pomona No.2 and No.1 Docks can be seen but have been in-filled. The area is ready for redevelopment, although at the time of writing building work has not yet commenced.

A little way past the location of the in-filled Pomona Docks is Woden Street Footbridge. The footbridge marks the boundary between Manchester Docks and the river Irwell. Before the docks were de-commercialised, it was also the lower limit of navigation for leisure craft.

The promenade alongside the river Irwell, looking towards Woden Street Footbridge.

The entrance to the river Irwell from the disused Hulme Lock. The river Medlock also joins the river to the left of the lock.

Care must be exercised if there has been a prolonged period of rainfall as the Irwell is narrow further upstream, and the passage of rainwater through the narrow section can be hazardous to navigation. It is prudent to make for Pomona Dock in these circumstances and await passage of Pomona Lock onto the safety of the Bridgewater Canal.

Nestling beneath the railway arches is the disused Hulme Lock, once the connection between the Bridgewater Canal and what is now the river Irwell. To the left of Hulme Lock entrance, hidden behind warehouses and factories, the river Medlock joins the Irwell after its subterranean journey beneath Potato Wharf and Castlefield Basins. James Brindley constructed a syphon to convey the Medlock from Deansgate, beneath the basins and wharves that he had built, to emerge a few hundred metres from the junction with the Irwell. Along the way, a subterranean chamber housed a water wheel, which powered winches to lift cargo from the canal level up to Deansgate. An overflow weir was also constructed at Potato Wharf in the shape of a giant cloverleaf. Over the years, successive developments have eaten away at the weir and only a small portion of it remains today.

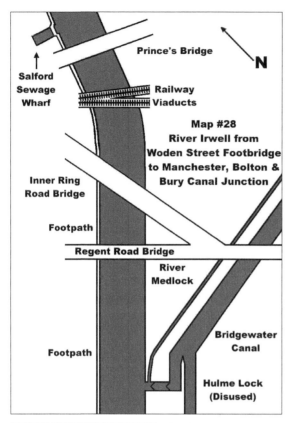

Prince's Bridge

N

Salford
Sewage
Wharf

Railway
Viaducts

Map #28
River Irwell from
Woden Street Footbridge
to Manchester, Bolton &
Bury Canal Junction

Inner Ring
Road Bridge

Footpath

Regent Road Bridge

River
Medlock

Bridgewater
Canal

Footpath

Hulme Lock
(Disused)

A barge entering Hulme Locks on its way to Manchester Docks.

Part of the site for the 1988 IWA Rally.

The entrance to the City of Salford's Ordsall Sewage Wharf during the IWA National Rally of Boats in 1988.

Narrowboats from Lymm Cruising Club moored outside the Mark Addy public house, May 2003.

A twin-arched road bridge, Regent Road Bridge, carries Regent Road across the river. This is followed by the new Manchester Inner City Ring Road Bridge. Shortly after the next two bridges, which both carry railway lines, the entrance to the Manchester, Bolton and Bury Canal can be seen on the left-hand bank. When excavations were taking place for the new ring road, work was held up where the ring road crosses the in-filled line of the Manchester, Bolton and Bury Canal while industrial archaeologists inspected the site. The ring road is carried across the line of the canal on bridges allowing full navigational height and width due to the proposed restoration of the canal.

The Manchester, Bolton and Bury Canal has many interesting features, including the Prestolees Aqueduct over the river Irwell, and the Wet Earth Colliery where James Brindley constructed drainage soughs for the mines and carried them beneath the Irwell in a syphon similar to that used for the Medlock at Castlefield, and later used extensively on the MSC.

Returning to the river Irwell, a twin-arched road bridge and two railway viaducts (one of which is the original Liverpool and Manchester Railway Viaduct), also with two arches, lie in close proximity to each other a little way upstream from the Ring Road Bridge.

Looking downstream towards Albert Bridge.

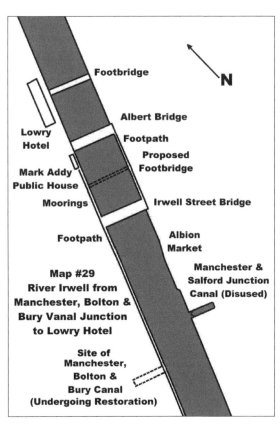

Footbridge

Albert Bridge

Lowry
Hotel

Footpath

Proposed
Footbridge

Mark Addy
Public House

Moorings

Irwell Street Bridge

Footpath

Albion
Market

Manchester &
Salford Junction
Canal (Disused)

Map #29
River Irwell from
Manchester, Bolton &
Bury Vanal Junction
to Lowry Hotel

Site of
Manchester,
Bolton &
Bury Canal
(Undergoing Restoration)

N

Immediately upstream from the three twin-arched bridges, adjacent to the Granada Television Studios, is another canal junction. This was the Manchester and Salford Junction Canal. This canal was built to break the Bridgewater Canal's monopoly on craft movements (and tolls) at the junction of the Rochdale and Bridgewater Canals, and between the two canals at Castlefield and the river Irwell at Hulme Lock. Little of the canal can be seen as it ran mostly in tunnels beneath the city, although part of it still remains beneath Granada Television Studios, and the original terminus with the Rochdale Canal can still be traced. The part beneath Granada Television Studios was used as an air-raid shelter during the Second World War, and the remains contain part of a lock. The left-hand riverbank on this stretch makes for a convenient mooring place with access to the city centre.

Albert Bridge is preceded by the Mark Addy public house. The pub is named after a man who, as a seven-year-old boy, was instrumental in the rescuing of an oarsman on the river close to Albert Bridge. In later life, Mark Addy saved fifty people from drowning. It is ironical that, during that period the Irwell was renowned for being contaminated with sewage and chemicals. Mark Addy died of poisoning after swallowing river water during his fiftieth rescue. The pub that bears Mark Addy's name also has moorings adjacent to it, serves excellent food and beers and is a convenient place from which to explore the city. A proposed footbridge is to connect the promenades on both sides of the river just below the Mark Addy public house.

Blackfriars Bridge with the cathedral in the background.

Looking downstream at Hunt's Bank... the limit of navigation, adjacent to the cathedral. Note the disused steps on the left to a long-gone landing stage. The nearest is Cathedral Approach, after which is Victoria Bridge.

After Albert Bridge, the river enters a concrete canyon punctuated by bridges and the occasional disused landing stage – a throwback to when passenger boats ran from the city. Albert Bridge is followed by Irwell Street Bridge, and Trinity or Calatrava Footbridge whose revolutionary suspension design connects the Lowry Hotel with the opposite bank of the river. Large office blocks loom over the river as Blackfriars Bridge is negotiated. After Victoria Bridge, the river is close to Manchester Cathedral, and only a few hundred metres of navigable river remain. The disused landing stage adjacent to the cathedral once gave access to the now sealed tunnels that run through the buried remains of 'Old Manchester' and lead to the cathedral's vaults. Beneath Salford Bridge is Hunts Bank, the head of navigation and the point at which it is time to turn around. Shallow-drafted craft can, in theory, navigate further upstream as far as the weir at Shooter's Bank, but this is not recommended due to the unpredictable nature of the river and the presence of submerged obstacles.

The journey that started from the river Mersey estuary at Eastham on the Wirral Peninsula, along the MSC, through the rolling Cheshire countryside and Manchester Docks, to the limit of navigation on the river Irwell in the heart of Manchester, is now complete. The journey has been one of many contrasts – from countryside to city centres and from marshlands to docklands. The MSC is a tribute to the Victorian entrepreneurs and engineers that had the vision, foresight and ingenuity to connect a city 40 miles inland to the sea, creating Great Britain's, and one of the world's, largest inland ports in the process.

The river Irwell, looking towards Woden Street Footbridge from Pomona Dock, May 2003.

A busy scene showing a Manchester Liner in No.9 Dock.

three

Navigational
Information

Pleasure craft wishing to navigate the MSC, Manchester Docks and the river Irwell can only do so by prior arrangement. When permission is granted it is usually to groups of pleasure craft that comply with strict safety and equipment standards, and possess certificates stating that they are seaworthy. Pleasure craft such as narrowboats are sometimes required to 'breast-up' (rope together) in case of engine failure and to aid stability in choppy water. The use of anchors is not allowed on the MSC, even though they are required for a Certificate of Seaworthiness.

The MSC is an extremely wide and deep commercial waterway. It is used by large coastal and quite often, very large, sea-going ships that can create a large amount of wash, even at low speeds. Sometimes, tugs accompany ships to help them manoeuvre around sharp bends on the canal. Even though leisure boating is timed to coincide with a lack of commercial traffic, care must be exercised at all times to prevent any disruption to the passage of any commercial craft encountered; after all; they are using the canal for business, not for pleasure.

If a large craft is encountered, keep well away from the canal's banks as the wash from the larger craft could deposit smaller craft onto the deeply shelving banks. Similarly, keep well away from the bow and stern of large vessel. Many modern ships feature submerged bows that protrude beneath the water line. They may also have bow-thrusters that can produce considerable turbulence when in operation. Besides the obvious hazards created by the vessel's propellers at the stern and their associated wash, it may have stern thrusters, which, when used in conjunction with bow thrusters, allow the vessel to move sideways. If there are small craft using the ship canal, larger craft usually wait until they have exited the section before proceeding.

When pleasure craft are using the canal they have to navigate a pre-determined route and adhere to a timetable as directed by MSC personnel, and are not permitted to deviate from this route or timetable. There are very few locations along the canal's length below Lowry Footbridge that are suitable for small craft to moor. It is, therefore, essential, in the interests of safety, that craft are in perfect operational condition so that there is no reason to moor along the canal unless at a pre-arranged location or under direction of the MSC personnel.

Access to the Welland Lock and Canal is currently strictly controlled by Salford Council, although it is planned to allow pleasure craft access through Welland Lock on the first weekend of the month during the summer period for a trial period. If this is well used, the arrangements for use of Welland Lock and the Erie Canal may change. Located in the base of Welland Lock's control tower is a sanitary station and water point, access to which is with the conventional BW key.

At its peak, the Manchester Ship Canal Co. operated the largest privately owned railway system in the United Kingdom. This photograph shows the Rolls-Royce-powered Sentinel diesel locomotive, No.3001, pulling a rake of chemical tankers.

Care must be exercised if there has been prolonged period of rainfall as many rivers empty into or share the ship canal's course. Locations where extra vigilance is required is at the following locations: the junction with the river Weaver where the current of water crosses the MSC to Weaver Sluices; the junction with the river Bollin where it empties into the ship canal; and Rixton Junction where the river Mersey enters the ship canal and the entire navigable length of the river Irwell. The river Irwell is narrow upstream and the passage of rainwater through the narrow section can cause the river's water level to rise significantly. This also causes an increase in the speed of the current. If there is prolonged rainfall and the river's water level rises, it is prudent to make for Pomona Dock and await passage of Pomona Lock onto the safety of the Bridgewater Canal. The large expanses of water contained within the ship canal, Manchester Docks and the river Irwell can be 'choppy' when the weather is windy.

The following is a list of wharves still in use along the length of the ship canal at the following locations:

Queen Elizabeth II Dock, Eastham	Oil and petro-chemicals
Manisty Wharf, Ellesmere Port	Bulk, semi-bulk and packaged cargoes
Ellesmere Port Docks	Bulk, semi-bulk, project and heavy lift

Stanlow Oil Docks	Oil for Shell UK's refinery
Stanlow Layby	Petro-chemical products, multi-user
Ince 'B' Berth	Certain petro-chemical products
Weston Point Docks	Salt and chemical products
Runcorn Saltworks	Bulk salt
Runcorn Layby	Petro-chemical and other approved liquid products with storage facilities and connection to ICI Runcorn
Wigg Wharf, Runcorn	Disused… formally the Guinness wharf
Walton Cut	Sand berth
Partington South Wharf	Bulk chemicals, LPG and petro chemicals for Shell, Montell and Nova Chemicals
Partington North Wharf	Petro-chemicals and other approved chemicals
Irlam Wharf	Dry-bulk, semi-bulk and general cargoes
Irlam Park Wharf	Scrap metals and other bulk cargoes
Cerestar Wharf	Private wharf supplying maize and other food products directly to the adjacent mill
Weaste Wharf	Cement to Blue Circle plant
Trafford Wharf	Barge wharf for grain to Rank, Hovis, McDougall
Manchester No.3 Dry dock	Commercial graving and dry docks and ship repairs

A busy night scene at the grain terminal at the end of Pomona No.9 Dock.

The maximum dimensions for craft using the ship canal are:

Eastham Locks:
Length: 182.88m (Large Locks) –   106.68m (Intermediate Locks)
Beam: 24.38m (Large Locks) –   15.24m (Intermediate Locks)

Above Eastham:
Length: 182.88m (Large Locks) –   106.68m (Small Locks)
Beam: 19.81m (Large Locks) –   13.71m (Small Locks)

Draft:
Up to Ince Oil Berth: 8.78m
Up to Runcorn: 8.07m
Up to Mode Wheel: 7.31m
Above Mode Wheel: 5.48m
Air draft above Runcorn: 21.33m

For further details and the latest navigational information, contact:

The Manchester Ship Canal Co.
Bridgewater House
Old Coach Road
Runcorn
Cheshire
WA7 1QT

Telephone: 01928 567465
Fax: 01928 567469
Email: mail@shipcanal.co.uk
Website: http://www.shipcanal.co.uk

There is an emergency telephone number for the Harbourmaster and Port Security at
Eastham: 0151-327-2212.

Footnote

I feel very privileged to be writing about canals and inland waterways at this time as it is a very exciting period for this subject. We are witnessing a new era with the redevelopment of Britain's canals and inland waterways as a leisure amenity.

There are many long-term restoration projects reaching fruition, such as: the complete rebuilding and subsequent reopening of the Anderton Boat Lift; the restoration and reopening of the Rochdale and Huddersfield Narrow Canals and Standedge Tunnel; the construction of completely new stretches of waterway like the Leeds and Liverpool Canal's Albert Dock Link in Liverpool; the Millennium Ribble Link which connects the southern end of the Lancaster Canal at Preston with the river Ribble, enabling a through route from the Leeds and Liverpool Canal to the Lancaster Canal via the river Douglas; the proposed restoration of the northern section of the Lancaster Canal; the continuing restoration of the Montgomery Canal; the construction of the Falkirk Wheel and the Millennium Link, completing a cross-country route across the Scottish Lowlands via the Forth & Clyde and Union Canals; the projected restoration of the Manchester, Bolton and Bury Canal; the possible reinstatement of Runcorn Locks, linking the Runcorn Arm of the Bridgewater Canal with the Runcorn and Weston Canal; the Cotswold canals such as the Thames and Severn Canal; plus many more projects too numerous to mention but, nonetheless important.

All these projects confirm that at last there is an awakening of both public and corporate awareness surrounding our forgotten heritage. This awareness is also confirming what canal boaters have known for many years – that the canals and inland waterways of Great Britain are amenities too valuable to lose, and should be cultivated, not forgotten and allowed to go to waste.

Not only are they examples of 'virtual history', providing an insight to how the transport system that fuelled the Industrial Revolution operated, demonstrating how our forbears worked and lived, but today provide a peaceful and (mostly) beautiful sanctuary from the pace and stresses of modern-day living. They also bring tourism – and hence money and investment – into areas of the country that would not otherwise benefit.

There are moves to bring back commercial freight-carrying of non-urgent cargoes to the canals and under-utilised waterways such as the Grand Union Canal and the river Weaver to name but two. This would require considerable investment to enable some routes to be reinstated to commercial status. I only hope that if this ambitious plan comes about it does not alter significantly the heritage aspect and character of our inland waterways system, which is a completely selfish statement. After all, what were the canals built for?

Let us also hope that the current interest and investment in the canals and inland waterways of Great Britain is not just a flash in the pan, but will continue to enhance our inland waterways system for future generations to enjoy.

Cyril J. Wood
July 2004

About the Author

Cyril Wood has had an active interest in canals and inland waterways since he was a child when, in 1960, his parents hired a cabin cruiser on the Shropshire Union Canal. He is an active member of Lymm Cruising Club and he and his wife Angie can be regularly found cruising their narrowboat *Total Eclipse* on the Bridgewater Canal and surrounding waterways.

Cyril is a qualified photographer and lecturer in photography. As well as being a prolific photographer and producing audio/visual presentations in his spare time, he has also written *The Duke's Cut: The Bridgewater Canal*, published by Tempus Publishing. Also in preparation is *Canalscape: Canal Cruising 1959 to 2005* (in three parts). Cyril has also written *Wyre Heal: A Local History of the Wirral Peninsula* as well as novels, photography text books and articles for many magazines on subjects ranging from photography, cine and video, multi-media, audio and hi-fi, Wirral's Local History, to canals and inland waterways of Great Britain. Many of these subjects are covered in his website which can be found at www.diarama.cwc.net, and Cyril can be contacted through Tempus Publishing.